Sleeper Cars
and
Flannel Uniforms

A Lifetime of Memories
from Striking Out the Babe
to Teeing It Up with the President

Elden Auker
with Tom Keegan

TRIUMPH
B O O K S
CHICAGO

Library of Congress Cataloging-in-Publication Data

Auker, Elden, 1910–
    Sleeper cars and flannel uniforms: a lifetime of memories from striking out the Babe to teeing it up with the president / Elden Auker with Tom Keegan.
        p. cm.
    Includes index
    ISBN 1-892049-25-2
        1. Auker, Elden, 1910– 2. Baseball players–United States–Biography. I. Keegan, Tom. II. Title.

GV865.A79 A3 2001
796.357'092–dc21
[B]   2001016165

This book is available in quantity at special discounts for your group or organization. For further information, contact:

Triumph Books
601 South LaSalle Street
Suite 500
Chicago, Illinois 60605
(312) 939-3330
Fax (312) 663-3557

Printed in the United States of America

ISBN 1-892049-25-2

Interior design by Patricia Frey

Contents

Acknowledgments

Elden and Tom would like to thank Nelson Braff and Tom Lasorda for introducing them and David Becker, M.D., for assisting with the book. Tom offers special thanks to Paul Coppini, English teacher at Bishop Kearney High School in Rochester, New York, for going the extra mile for every student fortunate enough to have sat in his classroom. Kudos to Tim O'Leary of O'Leary & Cosentino Communications, the best sports publicists in the business. Thanks to Tom Bast of Triumph Books for the title. Thanks also to Mitch Rogatz, Alex Simpson, Blythe Smith, and Angela Just of Triumph Books.

This book is dedicated to two beautiful women, Mildred Auker and Angie Keegan, and was written in loving memory of John F. Keegan, M.D., Tom's father and a great lover of baseball.

Introduction

My father worked hard for his money and didn't believe in spending it carelessly, even on his wide-eyed only child. We were out for a stroll one day when, as we approached the drug store, I told him I wanted an ice-cream cone.

"You do?" he asked. "Well, that costs a nickel, you know. Do you have a nickel?"

"No, I don't."

"I'll tell you what. If you really need an ice-cream cone, I'll buy you one. But if you just want one, then I don't think it's a good idea to buy one. If you spend your money on everything you want, you won't have any left over for the things you need. Now, do you need that ice-cream cone?"

"No, I don't," I answered

I'll never forget that lesson. I worked hard for my money, too, and I didn't go blowing it on ice-cream cones.

As a child my job was cleaning out the barn and milking the Holstein cow every morning and night. I didn't have any brothers or sisters, so that cow meant everything in the world to me.

My mother took care of bottling the raw milk, but it was my job to deliver it. We had a dozen customers on my milk route.

Some wanted it delivered in the morning; others wanted it at night. After Mom bottled the milk, I tucked the quarts neatly into the six-compartment wire carrier I had constructed in my Red Flyer wagon. The wagon had these cast-iron wheels that were about a half-inch wide. I'd put my foot over the outside, grab the handle, and use my foot to make it go faster, faster, faster, slapping the pavement to gain steam.

One particular evening I left home with the milk just as dusk was gathering. As I reached the corner where Mrs. Oliver lived, I started down the incline by her house. The front wheel of my little red wagon got caught in a crack in the concrete. I went over the top of the wagon. The wagon tipped to the side. The bottles flew. Every bottle hit the concrete and broke. Milk was all over the place. I skinned my knee and my elbow. The customers didn't get their milk, I didn't get the five cents we charged, and we had to buy new bottles. Those bottles were expensive, and we weren't made of money.

There I was on my skinned hands and knees, all alone in the dark, splattered with milk, picking up pieces of broken glass, putting them in the wagon, wondering if I could ever heal my fractured world. One minute I had it all: my milk, my bottles, my wagon. Then, in an instant, my world collapsed. Total devastation.

I cried all the way home over that spilled milk and didn't stop crying until I smothered myself in my favorite blanket, my mother's arms. She hugged life back into me, patted me, convinced me everything was going to be all right. You know how mothers are.

That was one of the most traumatic nights of my life, but I had learned a valuable lesson. It's important to take great care not to spill things, especially memories.

I have those tucked safely in the little red wagon between my "Mule Ears"—that's what Mickey Cochrane called me—and now the time has come to deliver them. I'm about the only one left who can. That's the toughest part about getting old. You lose everybody. Every time the phone rings you're afraid it's the daughter of another friend, calling to break more sad news to you, to remind you once more that nothing lasts forever.

Truth is, if I had known being a golf partner to Babe Ruth, a friend to Lou Gehrig, or teammates with Ted Williams, Hank Greenberg, Jimmie Foxx, Mickey Cochrane, Lefty Grove, and Charlie Gehringer was such a big deal, I would have written this book a long time ago. The more distant that era of baseball becomes, the more fascinating it seems to be to people.

Baseball wasn't such a big part of my life until I played for pay. Other than Babe Ruth, I don't know if I could have named another baseball player as a boy. When I was first called up from the minors, I didn't know whether the Tigers were in the American or the National League.

I pitched in the American League for 10 seasons, from 1933 to 1942, and twice pitched in the World Series for the Tigers. I can bring you into the clubhouse, on the trains, and into the hotel lobbies to let you see what it was really like. Or you can go on believing that we didn't care a bit about money and played only for the romance of it, go on believing that yesterday's players never had any personal problems. You can embrace all the misconceptions of pre–World War II baseball, if you like.

Or, you can turn off your cellular phone, remove the battery from your beeper, inform your personal trainer you won't be making it in this week, put on your slippers, settle back in your recliner, don your reading glasses, and take a trip back in time to visit with some of baseball's all-time greats.

I can take you behind the door of a hotel room in Detroit where Babe Ruth is beating up his roommate so badly that security had to be called to save the young ballplayer's life. Not that he didn't deserve to be pummeled. The thief. The lout. Keep reading and I'll let you in on the name of the man who stole from the Babe and nearly paid with his life. His unforgivable acts never made it into the newspapers and he went on to attain great celebrity in baseball, but we players all knew what he did.

I'll let you watch me pitch under an assumed name for a semi-professional team, something I had to do in order to retain my college eligibility. I was breaking the rules by accepting money to play. The most interesting of those games were two I played against the Kansas City Monarchs. I pitched against the great Satchel Paige in one of them.

You can have a front-row seat to some of the wildest temper tantrums in baseball history, thrown by Indians pitcher Wes Ferrell. And you can see what it was like to play for the best player/manager in the game, the fiery Mickey Cochrane, and his polar opposite, the nervous Joe Cronin.

Or join me aboard the *Marlin*, where, long after my playing days were over, my wife, Mildred, and I spent a most interesting day with Mr. Joe Kennedy. I'll share with you the chilling predictions he made about his three living sons and the memories he shared of his departed favorite, Joe Jr., while we were out at sea.

As big as the Kennedys were in Boston, it would take a living legend to match them in popularity—and a living legend Ted Williams was. Ted got a raw deal from the press in his early years in Boston and I'll take you back to the incident where that all started.

Anyone who thinks fame and fortune are immunizations against tragedy hasn't spent time around many celebrities. Ask Lou Gehrig, whose mysterious illness first spooked me when I snuck up behind him and grabbed him at Fenway Park. He fell to the ground and proceeded to tell me something was wrong with him, and he hadn't a clue what it was. Or ask Babe Ruth, who spoke with such a raspy voice the last day we spent together. Or Mickey Cochrane, driven to drink by the guilt he felt over the son with whom he never connected, the son who died in the war and was missed by Mickey every second of his life. Even Hank Greenberg, as nice a gentleman as you'd ever want to call a teammate, didn't have it so easy all the time. He kept most of it to himself, but there was the day the anti-Semitic taunts of an unidentified opponent drove him into the opposing clubhouse with revenge on his mind.

But most of my memories are good ones, whether forged on the diamond, at the card table, or on the golf courses of Florida in the off-season. We players were fierce competitors on the field, good friends off it. There was no trouble separating those conflicting feelings: one pitch under the chin in August, one great afternoon on the links in November.

I was voted All–Big Six at Kansas State in football, basketball, and baseball. The games have changed so much since then. I'll tell you how, if you'll just put down that damn cell phone.

You know, it's funny. I still get a lot of fan mail. That has changed, too. The letters used to say, "I watched you pitch." Then it was, "My dad watched you pitch." Now it's "My granddad watched you pitch." I haven't gotten any yet that say, "My great granddad watched you pitch." I'm looking forward to getting those. I'll read every one. For the moment, I'll write and you read. That way, you can learn what it was really like.

Chapter 1

An Underhanded Living

I didn't much care what was going on in major league baseball when I was a child, hunting squirrels with my cousin in Norcatur, Kansas. Sure, it was fun to play baseball, but why would I care what players were doing thousands of miles away when I was never going to see them anyway? I guess Babe Ruth was probably the only ballplayer whose name I would have recognized. Everybody was familiar with Babe Ruth.

Little did I know that the day would come when I would face Babe Ruth from only 60 feet and 6 inches away. I was a rookie pitching for the Tigers in 1933 and the Bambino was near the end of his career with the Yankees.

I was called in from the bullpen in the third inning. I had never been to Yankee Stadium and the walk in from the bullpen seemed as if it spanned four miles. Ruth watched from the on-deck circle as I took my warm-up tosses, underhand, as always.

I wasn't thinking about the fact that the biggest name in baseball's history was standing in front of me. I wasn't thinking about how he dominated the game in a way no man had ever before dominated a sport. I also wasn't thinking about the 60 home runs he hit in 1927, or the fact that in 1920—the year he brought back the game from the depths of the Black Sox scandal of 1919—he hit more home runs (54) than any other entire American League team. I viewed him the way I viewed any hitter, as a man I needed to get out. I struck him out on four pitches.

Next inning, as I was warming up, Art Fletcher, the Yankees' third-base coach who had a tough, lantern-jawed look about him, let me have it.

"Hey, bush, over here," he hollered. "Bush, bush, over here. Right here, bush. Look over here."

Finally, I snuck a glance in his direction and he was all over me.

"You got the Bam real upset," Fletcher hollered. "He's mad, all right. The Bam says he's been struck out plenty of times, but that's the first time he's ever been struck out by a damn girl!"

After the game I was sitting down in the locker room next to Tommy Bridges, my roommate. I told Tommy I was so mad at Fletcher that I wanted to grab a bat, storm into their locker room, and pretend he was a baseball.

Years later I mentioned the incident to the Babe when we were golfing at Bobby Jones Country Club in Sarasota. All the guys laughed when I told them what Fletcher had said to me. The Babe assured me that that was just Fletcher making up a story to get under the rookie's skin.

Of course I realized later that Fletcher was just doing his job. That's the way it was. Old-timers treated youngsters who came up unmercifully to try to rattle them. I became friends with Fletcher later in my career and told him I wanted to kill him that day. He turned out to be a pretty nice guy.

I didn't like being called a girl, but I wasn't about to change the way I pitched, either. It worked well enough for me to get to the big leagues at the age of 22.

I played football, basketball, and baseball at Kansas State, which at the time was known as Kansas Agricultural and

Mechanical College. In my first football game (as a sophomore against Purdue) I injured my shoulder in a way that is now referred to as a separation. That meant my days of throwing overhand were over; so, I learned to throw sidearm and did so throughout my college career.

After turning down a $6,000 offer from the Chicago Bears in order to sign with the Tigers for $450, I was convinced to drop my throwing motion down even further by Bob Coleman, my manager in Decatur when I was playing for the Class B Three-I League. Bob told me about Carl Mays, a submarine-style pitcher who won 208 games for the Red Sox, Yankees, Reds, and Giants from 1915 to 1929. Coleman said he caught him in the minor leagues and was impressed with how he was able to control his pitches compared to sidearm throwers.

"That plate is only 17 inches wide and you're trying to hit it from 60 feet, 6 inches," Coleman said. "Not too many pitchers can get it over consistently throwing sidearm. That target gets pretty small and you've got to get the ball over the plate if you're going to be a major-league pitcher. You're cutting your angle down when you're throwing sidearm. That's why the overhand pitchers are

Throwing underhand might have made Elden Auker rare among major-league pitchers, but he certainly wasn't unique.

"Iron Man" Joe McGinnity rode his submarine-style delivery all the way to the Baseball Hall of Fame. His underhand pitch was nicknamed "Old Sal." He won 20 games or more in each of the first eight seasons of a career spent mostly with the New York Giants, a career that started in 1899 and ended in 1908. He twice topped 30 wins in a season.

Carl Mays, who pitched for the Red Sox, the Yankees, and the Reds from 1915 to 1929, also came from down under. He won 207 games, yet is best known in baseball history as the only man to throw a pitch that killed a hitter, Cleveland shortstop Ray Chapman, in 1920.

Elden Auker loosens up with a catch before the game. *Photo from the personal collection of Elden Auker.*

more effective. I'd like to see you try throwing directly underhand. I'd like to see you line up with the plate, turn your rear to the hitter, and get your arm underneath. Then you have your control and all you have to work on is how high you're going to throw it because you're lined up."

I pitched batting practice for about five days throwing underhand and all the guys were moaning and complaining. Based on that, it seemed to be a pretty effective way to frustrate hitters.

Quincy, Illinois, which was leading the Three-I League (so named because the teams were all in Illinois, Indiana, or Iowa), was coming to town and Coleman told me he was going to start me in that game.

"I want you to throw underhand and I never want you to throw a ball any other way but underhand the whole game," he said. "I don't care how many hits you give up or how many you walk. I'm going to leave you in the whole game and I want you to throw every pitch underhand."

I tried it, beat them 1–0, and struck out 15 batters. I never again threw a pitch any other way. If not for Bob Coleman teaching me to come from down under, I probably never would have made it to the majors, and I wouldn't have been able to count some of the greatest men ever to play the game as such good friends.

I never felt compelled to apologize for making an "underhanded" living. But my style of pitching did lead to extra taunting, never more pointed than when delivered by Fletcher. It also led to opportunities that otherwise might not have come my way.

The unusual pitching motion landed me my first endorsement: "Submarine pitcher Elden Auker smokes Camels." They paid me $500 a year and sent me 12 free cartons of Camel cigarettes for lending my name to the product. They were so strong that they burned my throat up; I couldn't smoke them. I'd go to the grocery store near where we lived and the man who ran the store let me trade those Camels for my preferred brand, Lucky Strikes.

I quit smoking during the winter of 1942, not long after I quit playing baseball. I was working on the manufacturing of antiaircraft guns for the war effort and I was calling on buyers, master mechanics, and plant superintendents. The first thing I would do to start the conversation was pull out a cigarette, offer one, and smoke one myself. I was calling on so many plants that before I knew it I was smoking two packs of cigarettes a day and at night I was exhausted, felt lousy, and had a headache from smoking.

One of our salesmen, Mac McClure, died of a heart attack. I went to the funeral to say good-bye to Mac, and right in the middle of the service I had a terrible craving for a cigarette. I worked myself into a frenzy. I said to myself, "What the hell's the matter with me? These things have such a hold on me I can't concentrate. I can't even pay respects to my friend here without thinking I have to have a cigarette." Later, when we were walking out of the cemetery, I had a pack of Phillip Morris cigarettes with one left in it. I handed it to Louie Getshaw, our treasurer, and told him to take them because I was never going to smoke another cigarette for as long as I lived. I haven't had a cigarette in my mouth since that day.

I'm sure I would have been gone long ago if I hadn't made that decision. Now, looking back on my deal with Camels, I guess maybe I do owe an apology for making an "underhanded" living, but only for the $500 I received from the makers of Camels, not for the money I was paid for pitching for the Detroit Tigers, Boston Red Sox, and St. Louis Browns over the course of a 10-year career in the big leagues.

Chapter 2

Babe and Lou

Whenever someone finds out what I did for a living when I was in my twenties, they inevitably get around to asking about Lou Gehrig and Babe Ruth. And every time I'm asked about them, I think about what a shame it was that such nice guys came to such tragic endings.

I remember Opening Day, 1939: my first game playing for the Boston Red Sox after spending six seasons with the Detroit Tigers. The Yankees were in town.

With his back to me, Lou Gehrig had one foot up on the top step at the end of the tunnel that led to both clubhouses in Boston. He was smoking a cigarette, looking out onto the field. The guys who had been talking with him had just gone onto the field and he was about to do the same.

Gehrig, strong as an ox, was forever sneaking up behind people and hoisting them straight up into the air. This was my perfect chance to get him back, the way I'd been getting him back for the past six years. I snuck up behind him and slapped a bear hug on him. He instantly fell to the ground, offering no resistance whatsoever.

"Oh Elden, don't do that," he said, obviously in pain.

Elden Auker spent the 1939 season with the Boston Red Sox. *Photo from the personal collection of Elden Auker.*

Right then I knew something was seriously wrong. Gehrig was a pillar of strength and a great, good-natured guy who enjoyed little pranks like that. This wasn't the Lou Gehrig I knew.

"What the hell's the matter with you, Lou?" I asked after helping him back onto his feet.

"I don't know," he said. "There's something the matter with me. I'm so weak. I had a lousy winter and I couldn't hit the ball out of the infield all spring. I don't know what the devil it is, but something's not right."

Even as weak as he was, he was still in the lineup. He was determined to keep that streak going. We didn't know it then, but the streak was about to end at 2,130 games.

Later, in their season-opening road trip, the Yankees went to Detroit; from there Gehrig took a side trip to the Mayo Clinic near Minneapolis. It was there that he was diagnosed with amyotrophic lateral sclerosis, a disease that relentlessly attacks the nervous system. After his death on June 2, 1941, the disease became known as Lou Gehrig's Disease.

Gehrig played only eight games in 1939, and that day I snuck up behind him was the last day I ever spoke with him.

I also remember seeing the Babe 14 months before he died of throat cancer. His voice was so husky you could hardly hear what he was saying.

He came to Detroit on June 21, 1947. The Ford Motor Company was sponsoring American Legion Baseball in those days, and Henry Ford made Babe Ruth the honorary chairman for American Legion Baseball, paying him $50,000 a year to make appearances. Babe visited various Ford dealerships, did advertising for them, and visited American Legion teams all over the country.

Old Mr. Ford was way ahead of his time in so many ways. He didn't allow any smoking in the plant. Workers had to step outside to smoke, just like they do today. Even the great Babe Ruth had to step outside to smoke his cigar.

I reminded Babe about the day I first faced him, about how I struck him out and how hard Fletcher rode me for it. He said he remembered me telling him that story years earlier.

"That Fletcher, he was a real jockey, wasn't he?" the Babe said.

I had brought a picture I had of Babe for him to sign, and he was so taken with it that he wanted a copy for himself. We called up a reporter from the *Detroit Free Press* and he arranged for us to go down to the newspaper, where they made six duplicates of it for the Babe.

It was painful to hear him talking the way he did because he so loved to talk during his playing days.

Gehrig and Ruth's personalities were as different from each other as were their body types. As far as their personal relationship, I don't know anything about it except what I read in the newspapers, just like anyone else. They sure got along on the field during games though, I can tell you that.

Ruth was a very gregarious guy who loved life. He also loved to play golf. I played a lot of golf with him in Florida during the off-season. His wife, Claire, would drop him off at the golf course and pick him up after we finished our round. We played with Paul Waner, Wes Ferrell, Jack Russell, and Mickey Cochrane. We had a winter golf league for about three years.

Ruth was one of the most spontaneous, enthusiastic men you ever saw on a golf course. He had a great time out there. And he was the same way at the ballpark, always laughing and joking around. He called everybody "kid," except he pronounced it "keed." It was always, "Hey, keed." That way he didn't have to worry about remembering anybody's name. He knew everybody, even if he didn't bother to learn people's names, and everybody knew him.

Baseball's first commissioner, Judge Kenesaw Mountain Landis, made a rule that prohibited fraternization with fans. We weren't supposed to be talking to people in the stands. That was taboo. We were the actors, they were the audience, and there was to be no interaction between the two groups. That's the way Judge Landis wanted it. But Ruth paid no more attention to that rule than he did to the man on the moon. He was always waving to fans and walking over to the stands to start conversations with them.

While the Babe was flamboyant, Gehrig was a very quiet, reserved person. He lived with his mother for many, many years and took care of her until she passed away. He always had a smile on his face, a beautiful smile, but it wasn't nearly as loud a smile as Ruth's.

Ruth loved to drink and eat and he was always eating hot dogs before games. He liked to belch and pass gas and laugh about it. He was a big kid who loved life, a truly colorful character.

Claire traveled with Babe during his later years with the Yankees just to keep him in line. But nobody ever had to keep Gehrig in line. He was born in line and never stepped out of it. He was also an introvert, but if you knew him he was a friendly guy.

They both batted from the left side, but other than that they weren't much alike as hitters either. Gehrig was a solid contact hitter who had power. Ruth was more of a swinger than a pure hitter. He had remarkable power and you could strike him out more easily than you could strike out Gehrig.

Ruth had well-toned legs and was big from the waist up. He had broad shoulders, a thick chest, and a belly that hung over his belt. Ruth had a stronger upper body while Gehrig had a more powerful lower body. Gehrig, a couple of inches shorter than Ruth, had a big foundation with strong, powerful legs. His calves looked like little barrels. He had a small waist, no belly, and was all muscle.

Certain hitters you wouldn't dare throw at because to do so would be to wake them up. Ruth was one of those hitters. Other hitters you had to throw at to keep them from digging in at the plate. It was either throw at them or let them wear you out. That was your choice. Gehrig was one of those hitters.

I routinely threw at Gehrig's feet because that's where he dug in at the plate, with that big foot of his. Until I started throwing at his feet he wore me out.

He would holler at me, "Damn you, you're throwing at my feet, aren't you?"

I'd holler back, "What do you mean I'm throwing at your feet? If I want to hit you, I'll hit you in the head, where it won't hurt."

He got it in his head that I was throwing at his feet, which was exactly where I wanted to get—in his head, by way of his feet.

He was a lowball hitter and I was a sinkerball pitcher. I was pitting my strength against his and that was dangerous for me. It was hard for me to pitch him high. I couldn't keep it up and away from him. An overhand pitcher could pitch it high and keep it away from him. It was tough for me to do that because I was coming from down below.

Once I started throwing at his feet, I did much better. I'd get him to jump, get him to skip rope at the plate.

In those days there was no penalty for throwing at hitters. You could throw at anybody you wanted to throw at. On one particular afternoon I was throwing at Gehrig's feet while Bill McGowan was the home-plate umpire.

"Bill, he's throwing at my feet," Gehrig hollered to McGowan.

I hit Gehrig's toe with my next pitch and there he was: on his seat, rubbing his foot, cursing me, and saying I told you so to an umpire who didn't have an ounce of sympathy for him.

"Damn it Bill, I told you he was throwing at my feet," Gehrig said to McGowan. "He broke my toe." And I did break his toe, too. That didn't keep him out of the lineup, of course. Nothing kept Gehrig out of the lineup.

McGowan told Gehrig, "Ah, Lou, get up and get down to first base. Don't be such a baby about it."

His foot was killing him but he wasn't really mad at me. It was an accepted part of the game at that time and everybody from pitchers to hitters to umpires knew it. We were good friends and breaking his toe wasn't going to impact our friendship.

Both Ruth and Gehrig were as likeable as they were different from each other. It would take a real rat to do wrong to either one of them.

Chapter 3

Stealing from the Babe and Other Baseball Black Eyes

Imagine what this offer would bring on ebay.com: a chance to travel back in time to 1929 and become Babe Ruth's roommate for an entire Yankees road trip. What kind of bid would that bring at auction—$5 or $10 million maybe?

That's $5 or $10 million more than it would have brought from major-league players back then.

In '29, the Yankees couldn't pay someone to be the Babe's roommate. Not that he wasn't a nice guy. He was a very nice guy and treated everybody well. It's just that he wasn't an easy man to share a room with, not when you had to play a game the next day and needed your rest.

Babe was always carousing at night. He'd burst into the room in the middle of the night and start eating loudly, or worse. He was famous for drinking beer in his room, or worse. OK, no point in sugar-coating it, I guess: a big reason the Yankees had so much trouble finding a roommate for Ruth was his penchant for burping and passing gas. Some things a man just can't sleep through, and by all accounts, Ruth's gas was definitely one of those things.

The regulars on the team didn't want any part of rooming with the Babe, so the Yankees would always bring up a rookie and assign him to be Ruth's roommate. By the end of the road trip, the rookie could barely stand up, much less stand in against the best pitching he had ever seen.

Finally, the Yankees found a young shortstop who had what it took to withstand rooming with Babe and all his late-night interruptions. The kid made it through the first road trip and didn't utter a single complaint about his new roommate. The rook didn't show any of the normal signs of fatigue the others had shown. The next road trip arrived; they had the kid room with Ruth again, and again the roommate aired no complaints for the entire trip. The Yankees were convinced that they had finally found a roommate for the Babe and rid themselves of a nagging headache.

Then, during maybe the third trip the Yankees took with Ruth and his seemingly compatible new roommate, the Babe noticed he had been spending his money even more rapidly than usual. At the same time, some of the guys in the clubhouse noticed that they were missing some valuables, including money, watches, and rings.

This was very unusual; in that era, the sanctity of the clubhouse was such that I could lay a thousand-dollar bill on the floor on Opening Day and it would be there in the same spot, untouched by human hands, on the final day of the season. Fooling with a teammate's possessions was a taboo. Period. It just wasn't done. I would never have thought about reaching into someone else's locker to take anything, not even something as harmless as a bar of soap.

Ruth had more money than anyone on the team, so it was no surprise that he became the thief's No. 1 target. The Babe grew suspicious when he had to start checking for a hole in his pocket, he was spending his money so fast. Finally, when a gold pocket watch someone had given to him turned up missing, Babe decided to set a trap for the thief. He marked five $100 bills.

The Yankees were in town to play the Tigers (four years before I joined the team), and were staying at the Detroit Leland Hotel, where I first reported when I came up and where I first heard the story of how Ruth trapped and punished the thief.

Ruth came in at about 2:00 A.M., feeling good, and his sound-sleeping roommate was out cold. Ruth already suspected that his roommate might be the mystery crook, so he walked over to his roommate's bag and checked an out-of-the-way compartment in it. He found the five marked bills, and the gold pocket watch tumbled out and fell onto the floor. He pulled his roommate out of bed and proceeded to wipe up the room with him. He kicked the hell out of him so badly and made so much noise doing it that guests throughout the hotel awakened and alerted security.

Knocks at the door went unanswered as the power hitter continued to administer the beating the shortstop so richly deserved. Security unlocked the door and found that the big man in the room had beaten the little man seemingly to within inches of his life.

The Yankees did a magnificent job of keeping the story hush-hush and out of the newspapers, but people in Detroit, from the hotel to the clubhouse, knew exactly what had happened. The shortstop was sent back to New York the next day and was then released outright. Word spread throughout the American League that the released player was a no-good thief and he was black-balled from ever getting another job with an American League team. If not for the forgiving heart of Branch Rickey, the short-stop's career would have been over.

Mr. Rickey gave him a second chance and the thief went on to success as a player and then later as a manager. He became a well-known celebrity and was a big hit with the Hollywood crowd. His name: Leo Durocher.

He would become known as Leo the Lip, but I prefer to think of him as Leo the Lout. In time he became quite the hero in the eyes of the public; but nobody familiar with the cause of his banishment from the American League was even the slightest bit fooled by his phony charm. That included umpire Lou Coles, who hated Durocher.

I remember one exhibition game where Coles and Durocher came face-to-face. Something happened on the field that resulted in a controversial play. I forget what it was—whether it was a ball or strike call or a play at second base or something else. Whatever it was, Durocher charged Coles.

Coles stood up and said, "Get away from me you goddamn pickpocket. Don't speak to me."

I thought they were going to have to drag Durocher off the field in a straitjacket, he went so crazy. He jumped up and down, screaming and hollering. I thought he was going to haul off and hit Coles right there on the field.

"Get the hell away from me," Coles hollered at Durocher. "If you want to take a shot at me I'll be under the stands waiting for you." Of course, Durocher never went under the stands to meet him.

I'm sure Durocher hoped his past would never come back to haunt him; but once you steal in a baseball clubhouse, you're branded for life. He's lucky he ever got back in the game at all. He should have kissed the ground Branch Rickey walked on. He didn't, of course. Instead, he used him the way he used everybody else.

Mr. and Mrs. Rickey were nice enough to have Durocher over for dinner at their house one evening. They also invited Mrs. Rickey's seamstress to the dinner. She had a very successful business and made lots of money, more money than a shaggy-ass shortstop, which was all Durocher was. We used to call him the leather man. Lotta mouth, lotta hustle, good field, and no hit. He was a .247 lifetime hitter with no pop in his bat, the classic all-field, no-hit shortstop. Rickey loved players like that, loaded his roster with them. Guys like Pepper Martin. The St. Louis club was always a running team, a hustling team. The Gashouse Gang, free and easy and loose. They were a good, fun-loving bunch of guys for the most part.

The lout himself—Leo Durocher in 1934. *Photo courtesy of the Associated Press.*

Anyway, Durocher wasn't making any money to speak of, maybe $5,000. Mr. Rickey was tight with the buck. Mrs. Rickey's dressmaker, about 10 years Leo's senior, made a much better living. Leo ended up marrying her.

Rickey and Durocher were reunited with the Brooklyn Dodgers, where Durocher served as manager and part-time player. Durocher made the headlines, became a big star, and got rid of his wife, divorcing the woman who all but kept him before he made it big. He went Hollywood and started dating all the starlets.

While Durocher was with the Dodgers he would spend his winters in Hollywood, living with his best friend and his best friend's wife, Laraine Day. Durocher's penchant for stealing surfaced again, and this time he didn't stop at a gold pocket watch or cash. This time, he stole his best friend's wife.

Durocher's cheating ways finally caught up to him and led to him getting suspended by baseball's commissioner, Happy Chandler. Durocher and the well-known actor George Raft had a suite of rooms in the New Yorker hotel where all the ballclubs stayed. George Raft: now there was a real rat, a real lowlife. He and Durocher were the best of friends. They set up a gambling house in the suite, used a bunch of loaded dice and marked cards, and served free drinks. Dizzy Trout, a right-handed pitcher who replaced me in the Tigers' rotation when I went to the Red Sox, lost about $7,000 gambling there, virtually all the money he had. He was cheated out of it by Raft and Durocher.

Chandler launched an investigation, suspended Durocher for a year, and closed up the gambling joint. He should have kicked Durocher out for life.

I never had any use for Durocher, and you can lump Pete Rose in the same category, as far as I'm concerned.

Bud Selig and his successors should never even consider letting Pete Rose back in the game. In every major-league clubhouse there is a big sign about 3 feet tall and about 24 inches wide with great big print stating the rules of professional baseball. The No. 1 rule is no betting on the opposing team or on your own team. Those rules were posted in every clubhouse after the Black Sox scandal. Rose knew better. Baseball has ironclad evidence that Rose was betting on his own team, although he'll never admit it.

Tommy Lasorda introduced me to Bart Giamatti, and we once sat behind the dugout for an entire game. Giamatti loved baseball and was a brilliant man. Giamatti's people investigated Rose extensively. It's not like it was a spur-of-the-moment decision. Rose's own son once said he was the worst father any boy could ever have, and his first wife didn't paint a pretty picture of how he treated her, either. He didn't pay his income tax and they put him in jail for it. What kind of guy violates all the rules of society and of his profession? Now he sits around bellyaching because he can't get back in the game. Pete Rose is no good for the game of baseball. He's been a black eye to baseball, regardless of how good a player he was.

Rose doesn't have a sliver of an argument that he should be allowed back in the game. He signed the agreement that banned him for life and the commissioner had all the evidence against him. If Rose took his case to court, he wouldn't have a leg to stand on. He talks about wanting to sue baseball, but let him go ahead and try. The only thing he could accomplish would be making an ass out of himself.

If he does get in the Hall of Fame after he dies, and if justice is served, his plaque will sit on the wall right next to Durocher's, a rogues' gallery.

People try to compare Pete Rose to Shoeless Joe Jackson, but Jackson was vindicated by two juries. That showed he had nothing to do with the Black Sox scandal. Charlie Comiskey was the guy who should have been kicked out. The mob gave Jackson

$5,000; he took it to Comiskey, put it on his desk, and said, "Here, I don't want this money. I don't want in on this deal."

Comiskey said, "Get it the hell out of here. I don't want it. And keep your mouth shut."

Comiskey was afraid that if word of the bribe got out it would cause attendance to drop. He's the guilty man for not reporting it, for not standing up and protecting his player. Comiskey sat there and never said a word at the trial; he just let Jackson go down the drain.

Ask a baseball fan to name his favorite fiery manager and his favorite spirited ballplayer and many will answer Leo Durocher to the first question and Pete Rose to the second. Those wouldn't be my answers. I would have the same answer to both questions: Mickey Cochrane, my favorite player/manager.

Chapter 4

Mickey the Tiger

To know Mickey Cochrane was to admire him. He put so much passion and energy into everything he did. Whatever he touched on a baseball field seemed to turn into championship rings. He played in five World Series in all, three with the Philadelphia A's and two with the Detroit Tigers. He was a winner, a leader, and a Hall of Fame catcher. He twice was voted Most Valuable Player.

But Cochrane would have traded all that and more in half a second in exchange for one more chance at being a father to his son, Gordon.

Gordon Cochrane was shot and killed on the beaches of Normandy on June 6, 1944—now known as D-Day. The bullet that killed him had some kind of range. It traveled all the way across the Atlantic, lodged itself into the spirit of Gordon's father, the great Mickey Cochrane, and slowly killed him. Mickey's gravestone shows he died June 28, 1962, but he started dying June 6, 1944. Consider his another life claimed by World War II.

As if it weren't bad enough to lose a son in combat, Mickey suffered a double blow. Not only did he lose a son, he lost a son to whom he never considered himself much of a father. Gordon was a sickly child, always running at the nose, and burdened by asthma. As is often the case with sickly children, he was sheltered by his mother and became something of a momma's boy. He wasn't athletic in the least, and Mickey seldom brought him to the ballpark, feeling like he didn't have much in common with his son. Mickey and Gordon never really connected. Gordon outgrew his sickly ways and blossomed into a strapping young man in whom any father could take pride. But by then it was too late. Mickey had missed his chance to build a strong father-son relationship. He missed his son's childhood and there was no taking a mulligan on that.

Mary, Mickey's widow, told me that after Gordon was killed at Normandy, Mickey just went straight downhill, went to pieces. He was always so full of emotion. He was a sensitive man and just couldn't forgive himself for not building a better relationship with his son. Mary said Mickey started to drink heavily, trying to drown his guilty conscience. He developed cancer. The last time I saw him was at Yankee Stadium, in about 1960, when an old-timers game was organized between the Yankees and the Tigers. Mickey looked awful. His body had broken down and his spirit had been crushed. I never thought I would see the day that Mickey Cochrane's passion could be stripped from him.

For my money, Mickey Cochrane was the greatest player/manager in the history of baseball.

Bucky Harris managed the Tigers in my rookie season, 1933. He was a fine gentleman and a good manager, but I didn't learn what a truly great baseball manager could do to change a ballclub until a year later, when my career and the careers of all those around me were touched by genius.

Frank Navin and Walter O. Briggs owned the Tigers at the time. Mr. Navin was a fine gentleman and the picture of health, while Mr. Briggs was a paraplegic who became paralyzed from the waist down after contracting syphilis. Mrs. Briggs was a wonderful gal, but her husband was such a cold man that even his wife had to make an appointment through Briggs's secretary, Jo Shevlin, just to see her husband.

Mr. Briggs had the money and it was up to Mr. Navin to convince him to spend it. He convinced old man Briggs to spend it wisely in the winter before the 1934 season. Connie Mack, the famous owner and manager of the powerhouse Philadelphia A's, was getting hounded by creditors during the Great Depression and had to dismantle his ballclub to pay his bills. Mack traded Cochrane to the Tigers for Johnny Pasek and $100,000, and Cochrane was named player/manager. With that one move, we were transformed from a young team unsure of itself into a confident, aggressive championship contender.

Mickey Cochrane was the perfect player and the perfect manager in the perfect situation. He was just what the city of Detroit and the Tigers' organization needed. The Tigers had not won a pennant in 25 years and badly needed someone to show them how to do it. In Cochrane, who had already played in three World Series for the A's, the Tigers found that man.

We all met Mickey on the first day of spring training in 1934, the first spring the Tigers trained in Lakeland, Florida, instead of Tucson. Right away, it was obvious to all of us that this man was something special. He was a natural born leader.

We had finished fifth the year before with a losing record. We had some talent, but we were too young. We had Hank Greenberg at first base, Charlie Gehringer at second, Billy Rogell at short, and Marv Owen at third. In the outfield, we had just gotten Goose Goslin from the Senators to go with Gee Walker, Jo Jo White, and Pete Fox. Cochrane caught against right-handers and Ray Hayworth, who was the starting catcher the year before, caught against left-handers. Cochrane was the dean of the group. Tommy Bridges and Schoolboy Rowe were our top starting pitchers.

We held meeting after meeting; Cochrane talked in a way that held our attention. He would stand up and start talking to us about confidence and about playing in the World Series and what it was like to win the pennant, how great a feeling it was. The more he talked, the more charged up everybody got.

A few weeks into spring training, he stood up and said, "We've got a ballclub here that can win a pennant. I know. I've played for pennant winners and I'm telling you this ballclub is as good as any ballclub I've ever seen."

At first we didn't know what to make of that, and were looking at each other thinking he must be crazy or something. We thought of ourselves as just a bunch of young guys who had finished in the middle of the standings, and now he was comparing us to the A's of Al Simmons, Jimmie Foxx, and Lefty Grove? At first we thought, "What the hell is this guy talking about?" But by the end of the meeting, we started believing it.

"We've got the best pitching I've ever seen," he told us. "This pitching staff is better than the pitching staffs I caught in Philadelphia. We've got the best first baseman in the league. We've got the best second baseman in the league. We've got the best double-play combination in the league. We've got six or eight .300 hitters. We can win the pennant."

We started believing it and we started playing like we believed it. We played those exhibition games as if they were the seventh game of the World Series. We held nothing back. As a team, we took on the spirited personality of our manager.

It didn't take Cochrane long to win over the pitching staff. He gathered us all together and told us what he expected of us as pitchers.

"Look," he said. "I want to explain myself. I'm the catcher on this team and I'm also the manager. But when you're on that pitcher's mound, that ballgame is your ballgame. Never, I mean never, throw a pitch to me you feel like you don't want to throw. I don't give a damn what the situation is in the ballgame. If I call for a certain pitch and you don't feel like throwing that pitch at that time, then you shake me off. I'll take the credit when we win the ballgame, but if you lose the ballgame, it's your fault. Losing is a lot easier to live with if you know you've given it your best shot, so go with the pitch you want to go with, not the pitch anybody else thinks you should throw."

Bridges was 27, Rowe was 24, and I was 23, and here was the great Mickey Cochrane, former American League MVP, from the great Philadelphia A's, telling us we were in charge of our games and that when we had the baseball in our hand we didn't have to defer to anybody, not even him. You think hearing that didn't bolster our confidence? Empowered by the manager, we took our pitching to an entirely different level. Schoolboy had won seven games the previous season. He won twenty-four in '34. I won three games in '33 (after being called up from the minors) and fifteen in '34. Bridges never had won more than fourteen games in a season. He won twenty-two in his first season pitching for Cochrane.

Six of our eight regulars batted .300 or better and we finished the season with a .300 team batting average. It was Cochrane, not Triple Crown winner Lou Gehrig, who was voted Most Valuable Player of the American League that season. One year after winning 75 games, we won 101 and finished 7 games ahead of the second-place Yankees.

Cochrane convinced us from the start that we belonged on the same field as any team, even the mighty Yankees of Ruth and Gehrig, Bill Dickey and Tony Lazzeri, Lefty Gomez and Red Ruffing.

When we went to New York for our first series of the year against them, Mickey had us all fired up. He told us not to speak to any of the Yankees. He told us to get mean.

"We're not here to make friends," Cochrane told us during a clubhouse meeting before the series. "We're here to whip the hell out of them."

For him, to talk with such confidence when the opponent was the Yankees gave us all a belief in ourselves we never had experienced. That's when we knew we could win the pennant.

Cochrane kept us fired up all year and we never let down. Rowe had his sharp curveball working so well he didn't lose a game from June 15 through August 24. He reeled off 16 consecutive victories.

Mickey carried the fight on the field by the way he ran the bases, the way he blocked the plate, and the way he battled pitchers with a bat in his hands. He always kept the bench going, always made sure everyone who wasn't playing in the game was into the game mentally, emotionally, and vocally.

His .320 lifetime batting average was a record for a catcher, and defensively, in his ability to handle pitchers, nobody performed better. He knew his pitchers so well that he had a knack for knowing exactly the pitch they wanted to throw in every situation.

Mickey was a master psychologist. He used completely different motivational methods depending on the personality of the player. Schoolboy Rowe could do no wrong as far as Mickey was concerned. Schoolie would get knocked out of the box and Mickey would slap him on the back and tell him, "We'll get them next time. Don't worry about it. I know you'll shut them down next time."

He treated me just the opposite. He seldom complimented me after a game. No matter what I did, he told me how I could have done it better. He rode me all the time. His philosophy was to try to keep me mad. I guess he thought I pitched better when I was in a nasty mood.

"The only reason I even keep you around is so that I won't have the biggest ears on the team," he told me. He called me Mule Ears and it didn't bother me. That was just Mickey, trying to make me angry, as usual.

I'll never forget one day when I faced Cleveland's Mel Harder, the pitcher I opposed more than any other during my

Elden Auker with Mickey Cochrane, left, in 1935. *Photo from the personal collection of Elden Auker.*

career, and beat him 2–1. I allowed four hits. Sam Rice, who spent 19 seasons with the Senators, was with the Indians for the last season of a career that included only 34 home runs. He was a little slap hitter who couldn't have weighed more than 150 pounds, soaking wet. He would stand up there flat-footed and punch the ball around. He could barely hit the ball out of the infield and he got three of the four hits off me that day.

Mickey's locker was right next to mine in Cleveland. While Mickey was outside talking to the sportswriters, all the guys stopped by my locker to tell me, "Great game, 'atta boy, way to go, Auk," the usual compliments you hear after pitching a good ballgame and getting the win. Mickey came walking in with his mask perched on the top of his head the way it always was. He was wringing wet with sweat and his face was dirty from a day of catching in the hot sun. He took off his chest protector and threw it in his locker. He started to unbutton his shirt and he looked at me and said, "When the hell are you ever going to learn how to pitch to Sam Rice? For crying out loud, you can't get him out to save your life and he can't even hit the ball out of the infield against anybody else. What's the matter with you?"

That's just the way he was with me. I didn't take it personally and we remained great friends. I loved the guy like the brother I never had. We socialized in the off-season, and my wife and I were great friends with Mickey and his wife. We played bridge together. Mickey and I went quail shooting, fishing, and golfing together. But once the season started, he was the manager and I morphed back into the player whom he treated the most harshly. That didn't put the slightest strain on our friendship; it was just accepted that, in our profession, that was the way it was.

Cochrane used a little trick to motivate pitchers who started to show signs of fatigue late in a game. He made a signal from behind the plate to the bench to have a reliever start warming up in the bullpen. He made sure the starting pitcher saw the signal, which made us give it everything we had left to stay in the game. In those days, not completing your own game was something of an insult. It was a very effective little ploy on his part.

He was such an outgoing guy that he had friends throughout baseball, even among the umpiring crews. He carried his friendship with umpire Bill McGowan a little too far for my taste one day in St. Louis. We were beating the Browns 10–0 and I was closing in on a shutout. Cochrane and McGowan apparently grew bored with the one-sided game and were having a grand time swapping stories. It was as if Mickey was sitting back in his rocking chair on a lazy afternoon. McGowan was so rapt by Mickey's stories he called a pitch right down the pike a ball. That triggered my temper. I stormed off the front of the mound.

"Listen, if you guys want to have a picnic, why don't you take those uniforms off?" I hollered.

McGowan said to Mickey, "What's the matter with him anyway?"

Mickey, without a care in the world, said, "Ah, don't pay any attention to him."

It worked. They started paying attention and I went on to finish one of my 14 career shutouts and 126 career complete games.

When he felt he had to, Mickey came down hard on players. He suspended Walker for not hustling but left the ultimate decision up to the team. We backed Cochrane after he asked, "Do you want this guy to take money out of your pockets?"

Walker gave Cochrane fits. He was a good hitter and he was fast but he was reckless on the bases. Mickey didn't have any rules for base runners and thought it was best to let them decide when to try to steal a base. He turned them loose and gave everyone the green light all the time. Most of the guys had the sense not to abuse that privilege. Walker would try to steal bases whenever he felt like it. He went through a streak where he repeatedly got picked off first base. Walker was picked off base twice in one series in Detroit; the second time, it cost us the ballgame.

Cochrane fumed over it. He was as angry as I had ever seen him. He held a special meeting to implement a new regulation at the start of a road trip to St. Louis, the first game after Walker had cost us the game.

"You guys are getting caught off base and I'm getting tired of that," Cochrane told us. "There's no damn reason for it. We lost a ballgame in Detroit because of it and I've had it. It's not going to happen again. I'm making a new rule. From here on out, anybody who gets caught off base, it's a $50 fine."

Jack Knott, a pretty good pitcher, was on the mound for the Browns that day. Cochrane got a hit his first time up and, wouldn't you know it, Knott caught him off base. I don't think Mickey Cochrane ever had anything tougher to do on a baseball field than that particular walk back to the dugout. He came in with his head down. His face was fire-engine red. He was cussing all the way back to the dugout. He was blaming Knott. He was blaming the umpire. He was blaming everybody under the sun. Boy, was he boiling mad. He put his shin guards on with such fury that he just about pulled the straps off. We didn't dare say anything. We were all too afraid to utter a sound. Dead silence. But after a while we couldn't hold it in anymore, and we all started laughing.

Finally, Mickey started laughing. He turned around and said, "You bastards, you. All right. Give it to me. I deserve it." We gave it to him. And he paid his $50 fine.

We won the pennant under Cochrane in 1934 and won the World Series with him leading the way in 1935. But the pressure of trying to maintain that level of success got to him to the extent that he had a nervous breakdown in 1936 and had to leave the team in midseason. He went to Wyoming to recuperate and was

Mickey Cochrane, second from left, with his 1935 starting rotation: Schoolboy Rowe, Elden Auker, Tommy Bridges, and General Crowder. *Photo courtesy of the Associated Press.*

his old, spirited self when he returned to lead us through a late-season surge that pushed us past the White Sox and Senators and into second place. We were no threat that year to the Yankees, who finished first by 19½ games.

I honestly think we would have won it all in 1937 but for losing Cochrane on May 25 to a life-threatening beaning in New York. Bump Hadley of the Yankees hit Cochrane on the head with a pitch that was punctuated by the most frightening sound in all of baseball: the noise made when a baseball hits the head, a sound always followed by a heavy, prolonged silence. I joined several teammates in carrying Mickey off the field. His skull was fractured in six places. His playing days were over. That took the life right out of us. He returned to manage much later in the season, but it wasn't the same. Cochrane was born to be a player/manager. He had to be out there in the middle of the fire, leading by example, to be at his best.

Mickey spent only four of his thirteen seasons with the Tigers, but he went into the Hall of Fame as a Tiger, not as a representative of the A's. It was only right. Mickey was a Tiger in every sense of the word.

His playing and managing days long behind him, Cochrane received a Naval Commission to coach the Great Lakes Naval Base team. They earned a great deal of acclaim in 1944 by winning 33 games in a row, finishing with a 48–2 record, and beating the Cleveland Indians 17–4 in an exhibition. It was also the worst year of Cochrane's life, thanks to D-Day.

It was terrible that Mickey put himself through so much pain, blaming himself the way he did. He deserved a better fate. He exuded such spirit, such class, such dignity. In time he would have become close to Gordon. He just never got the chance.

But most of my thoughts about Mickey bring a smile to my face. He commanded so much respect from us. As I've mentioned, he didn't have many rules, but I do remember one of them. Among the first words out of his mouth as player/manager of the Tigers were: "I expect you guys to conduct yourselves like gentlemen. You are to wear a coat and tie at all times. Never come to the ballpark without a coat and tie. If you do, you're out $50. If I catch you in the hotel dining room without a coat and tie on, it will cost you $50."

We dressed first class. We played first class. As a reward for that, the Tigers made sure we traveled first class.

Chapter 5

All Aboard
the Tiger Special

C lick, click, click, click, click, click, click. Nothing quite like the sound a train makes purring through the night, eating miles peacefully, swiftly, reliably. You hear that soothing sound and there's no mistaking it for any other. An automobile's horn makes you jump. A jet's roar makes you flinch. But a train's click makes you relax. Taking the train was the only way to go. It's a far more comfortable way to get from city to city than the airplane.

No train could compare to the Tiger Special, our very own team train. Its schedule was simple: when we were ready to go, it was too. Michigan Central Railroad set it up for us when we were driving for the pennant in 1934. It was first-class all the way. It had all the modern amenities, all the luxuries. No team traveled in more comfort than the Detroit Tigers.

When it was the final day of a homestand or the final game in a particular city, we would slip out of our flannel uniforms, shower and dress, tie our ties, slip on our sport coats, don our hats, then get onto the train and jump into our berths. We were the closest bunch of men you ever saw, and traveling together by train did nothing but draw us closer. We loved each other like brothers. We traveled together, we slept together, we ate together, we played together, and we fought together.

Playing together and doing what was best for the team during the course of a game never was an issue. It was just the way it was done. Nobody thought about his individual statistics. Imagine how uncomfortable it would have been for a player to play for his own glory at the expense of a win and then get on a train (which was like sharing a house) with the players he had stolen a victory from. It just didn't happen. Nobody would do it because nobody would want to feel the wrath of 48 eyes burning down on you. I can't speak for all the players, but I can say that I always enjoyed riding the trains.

We passed the time playing cards: hearts, bridge, or poker. When it came to dealing the cards, General Crowder was in a class by himself. Crowder joined us late in the '34 season at the age of 35. He was having a rough year with Washington and some people probably figured he was washed up. If so, they figured wrong. He won 4 and lost 10 for the Senators. Once he joined us, his career was rejuvenated. He won 5 and lost 1 in 9 starts for us down the stretch. He helped us, and not just on the field. He made the train rides more interesting, too. He showed us card tricks but

Once upon a time, a baseball player would stand out if he didn't have a nickname. Consider the World Champion 1935 Tigers: Elon Chester Hogsett went by Chief Hogsett. Henry George Schuble answered to Heinie. Alvin Crowder was better known as General Crowder. Gerald Holmes Walker was Gee Walker. Lynwood Thomas Rowe was never called Lynwood. He was called Schoolboy. Ervin Fox went by his middle name, Pete. Joyner White was Jo Jo White. Ralph F. Perkins was better known as Cy Perkins. Gordon Stanley Cochrane answered to Mickey. Nobody called Herman Clifton by his real name. They called him Flea. And Leon Allen Goslin went by the name of Goose.

never used them to cheat us out of money. He would never cheat a teammate. That just wasn't done.

Card playing was in Crowder's blood. He was weaned on it. He had an interesting background and grew up in a hurry. He was a professional gambler as a kid. He worked in a gambling house and a "house of ill repute" as a youngster in North Carolina. He was a runner for the girls and the gamblers. If they needed drinks, he got them drinks. He ran himself ragged doing errands for the men in the gambling room and the women in the, ahem, bedroom. Whatever they needed, he did it for them. In return, he said they looked after him, made sure no harm came to him. He never engaged in any sort of sexual relationship with them, or if he did he never shared that with us.

There were seldom any incidents on the train, but things got quite heated between Rudy York and "Boots" Poffenberger once during a poker game on the train in 1937 or '38. Rudy York was a very powerful man and a real gentleman who never bothered anybody and didn't talk a great deal. Boots Poffenberger was just the opposite. Boots Cletus Elwood "the Baron" Poffenberger had a long name and short arms. He was a chunky little right-handed pitcher. He was always talking and was quite the ladies' man.

Boots was from Williamsport, Maryland, and enjoyed making the trip to Philadelphia to play the A's. Manager Mickey Cochrane had given us an 11:00 curfew. Everyone had to be in his room by 11:00 P.M. One night in Philadelphia, Poffenberger not only missed curfew, he missed it by a lot. He didn't get in until about 3:00 A.M.

The next day, Cochrane held a special team meeting to discuss Poffenberger's curfew violation. "Boots, we have a curfew on this team, you know," Cochrane said.

"Yes sir, I know," Boots said.

"You're supposed to be in at 11:00," Cochrane said.

"Yes sir, I know," Boots said.

"Where were you last night when you were supposed to be in your room?" Cochrane asked.

"Mr. Cochrane," Boots said, "I refuse to reveal my whereabouts."

We all fell over laughing at that remark, and so did Cochrane. That was the end of the meeting and Poffenberger wasn't punished.

But Boots didn't get off so easily when he triggered York's temper during that poker game on the train. York was trying to mind his own business playing poker. Poffenberger wouldn't let him. Boots wasn't playing. He was just staring over York's shoulder, watching him play. At the end of each hand, Boots would tell Rudy you should have done this, you should have done that.

York had heard enough of it. "Boots, if you don't shut your mouth, I'm going to throw your ass off this train," York told him.

They played a few more hands and Boots again offered his opinion on how York had misplayed. York picked up Boots, put him under his arm, walked to the door between one car and the next, and was going to throw him off the train. Boots was kicking and screaming and York couldn't get him through the door. Finally, York let him down. That scared the hell out of Boots. He didn't say another word and York was able to play poker in peace.

But incidents such as that were rare. For the most part, riding the trains was all about relaxation and strengthening friendships. We spent so much time together traveling from one city to the next by train that it didn't take long for a new player, such as Crowder in 1934, to feel like part of the team, part of the family. The wives never traveled with us. Nobody came between us. Our bond grew forever stronger.

We had great school spirit and team spirit during my college days at Kansas State. It's not easy to top that kind of spirit at the professional level. But the Detroit Tigers of 1934, 1935, and 1936 did. I can honestly say the team spirit we had in those years was greater than any I have ever experienced. I never saw anything like it before or after.

If someone dove in the outfield to catch a ball, we all held our breath until he got up and showed us he was all right. If one of us pitchers got our ears knocked off, gave up three or four runs in the first inning, everybody felt bad.

Some of the train rides were long ones, yet never so long that we got on each other's nerves.

We were so close that many of us even made a point of trying to live near each other in Detroit. Tommy Bridges, Ray Hayworth, Chief Hogsett, Gerald Walker, Jo Jo White, and myself lived in the same complex with our families. The six of us would get into two cars and drive to the ballpark together every day. You might think that after all the time we were forced to spend together on the job—in the clubhouse, on the field, on the trains—we would try to avoid each other during what little

Elden Auker and Chief Hogsett rest for a moment in the Tigers dugout. *Photo from the personal collection of Elden Auker.*

free time we had to spend during a season, but that wasn't the case at all. We enjoyed each other's company.

Players filled the first two Pullman cars of the Tiger Special. The Pullman cars were built with upper and lower berths. The upper berths always remained empty. We used only the lower berths. The players' dining car was located after those first two cars. The baggage car, which carried our bats and balls, gloves and spikes, uniforms and clothes, was located behind our dining car.

The press car was behind the baggage car. I hear all sorts of stories now from writers talking about the good old days when they were friends with the players and would play cards with them on the trains. I hear those stories and I shake my head. I can't speak for how it was with other teams, but I can tell you unequivocally that on the Tigers' train we never saw a man from the press when we were on the train. That was our time to be by ourselves. The sportswriters would interview us at the ballpark and sometimes even at our hotel. Never on the trains. It was understood that just wasn't done. We never went back to their car and they never came up to ours. The writers' club car was stocked with liquor for the sportswriters to have their drinks. For some reason, many of the writers drank a lot. They drank all the time. Many of them drank far too much, they really did.

We came to know the porters on the Tiger Special quite well and developed friendships with them. Most of the porters were baseball fans and they loved to travel with us. They fought for those jobs as porter on the Tiger Special. It was a status symbol to be able to say you were a porter for the Detroit Tigers. We always had the best porters. They would do anything for us, no matter the time of day or night. They shined our shoes for us. They made our beds in the sleeper cars. The service on the Tiger Special was top of the line. They fixed us whatever we wanted to eat whenever we wanted to eat it.

The dining room was open 24 hours. The same chef and waiters always traveled with us. If they were sleeping, they would wake up the second we walked back there. They would get up and fix us whatever we wanted. If one of us wanted a steak at midnight, they would get up and fix it just the way we liked it and they would be happy to do it.

Even in the middle of the night, if I walked back there and they were sleeping, they would get up right away, pleasant as can be, and say, "Yes sir, Mr. Auker, what will you have?"

"I'll have a bowl of Grape-Nuts with a scoop of chocolate ice cream on it, please," I would say. I can still taste that bowl of grape nuts with a scoop of chocolate ice cream. It was my favorite. It still makes my mouth water. Or I would order another favorite snack of mine: a half a head of lettuce in a bowl with Thousand Island dressing and toast. It got to where they knew just what you liked and just how you liked it.

The dining room was also a favorite hangout when we weren't sleeping. If I had pitched a ballgame that day and was still hot at night, I'd go back to the dining room to cool down for a while.

This was our train and ours alone. It didn't have to stop until it got to where we were playing our next series. It would shoot past cities at night, whistle blowing, giving us that sound you got nowhere else, that sound that lulled you to sleep: click, click, click, click, click, click, click. Click, click, click, click, click, click, click.

The Tiger Special took us as far east as Boston and as far west as St. Louis. It took us to all the stops in between: to New York, Philadelphia, Washington, Cleveland, Chicago. And it took us back home to Detroit, where the city's fine baseball fans came out every day to support us as few other cities supported their team.

The Tiger Special took us all the way to the pennant, all the way to the World Series, where the Dean brothers, Dizzy and Paul, and the rest of the Gashouse Gang awaited us for a wild Fall Classic packed with drama.

Chapter 6

Me 'n' Paul

Dizzy Dean had one of the greatest names in baseball and was one of the greatest pitchers of all time. And as far as marketing genius is concerned, old Diz didn't need to take a back seat to anybody. He was way ahead of his time in that regard.

Dizzy had two personalities. He let his friends and family see the real one. The rest of the world saw the more colorful Dizzy Dean, the one the media has preserved for eternity. In reality he was as refined a gentleman as I ever looked at from across the table. That's right, refined.

There was no mistaking who ran the Dean household, and it wasn't Dizzy. His wife, Pat, did not allow any liquor in the house. No beer, no whiskey, no nothing. They had Coca-Cola and if you wanted a drink, well then that's what you had to drink. When Diz was at home he was quite the host. He was the most quiet, mannerly guy you ever saw.

Pat would tell him, "Go get this, Diz."

His response to her never wavered. "Yes, love," he always said, before carrying out her instruction.

She always called him Diz. She might have called him Jerome when she got mad at him for all we knew. But she never got mad at him in front of us. And as compliant as he was with her, I doubt he ever gave her reason to become angry with him.

Dizzy was most articulate in his speaking and very refined in his actions. He was the same way when the players who lived in Florida during the winter got together for golf. He was a well-mannered, proper gentleman and as intelligent as a man could be. If his golf swing had been as smooth as his manner of speaking, he could have broken par on every round.

I don't know if Dizzy ever broke 90 when he first picked up the game, but if there was money on the line, he could beat just about anybody. He was some competitor. In time he became a pretty decent golfer.

It was the same with his public persona. Dean knew he could make more money being old Diz than being Jerome Dean, so old Diz he was.

Dizzy Dean, Elden Auker, and Babe Ruth at the first Professional Baseball Players' Golf Tournament in January of 1935. *Photo from the personal collection of Elden Auker.*

Falstaff Brewery signed him to a lifetime contract and used many of his colorful expressions to promote Falstaff beer. I never did see Dizzy drink a beer, certainly not at his house anyway, but he was happy to say he drank Falstaff regularly. He wasn't only a great pitcher, but a great pitchman.

As soon as a sportswriter came around, Dizzy became a different person. He went right into that crazy Southern slang that he had. He would give them one of those, "Hey pardner, how y'all doing?" greetings. He really laid it on thick, played it to the hilt, and they always bought it hook, line and sinker.

Years later, when I would see him on television, he told great stories in that exaggerated Southern drawl of his. He had some great stories to tell about when he first came to the major leagues. He also shared with us some of the trials and tribulations of growing up as the son of a sharecropper. He moved about the South, working the fields, harvesting crops.

Dizzy Dean certainly did have an interesting background. He didn't have to fabricate any of that. It was more in the delivery that the embellishment came into play. As a broadcaster, Dizzy wouldn't say, "He slid into third." He certainly knew that was the proper way to say it. It just wasn't the most lucrative way. He preferred to say, "He slud into third."

On the eve of the 1934 World Series against us, Diz predicted that the Cardinals would win and that he and his brother Paul would get all four wins. "Me 'n' Paul will win 'em all," he said, or something to that effect. Well, he had T-shirts made up that said "Me 'n' Paul" and he made more money off those T-shirts than the St. Louis Cardinals paid him to pitch for them. He said making a prediction "ain't braggin'" if he could back it up. He and Paul backed it up. Dizzy went 30–7 in the regular season that year and made 17 of his 50 appearances out of the bullpen.

We had the more powerful lineup, with four hitters who drove in 100 runs: Hank Greenberg (139), Charlie Gehringer (127),

Goose Goslin (100), and Billy Rogell (100). Our infield of Greenberg, Gehringer, Marv Owen, and Rogell combined to drive in a record 462 runs.

The Cardinals were a scrappy bunch of hustlers, just the sort of players Branch Rickey loved to make a team out of. They were some of the loudest bench jockeys the game ever saw. Rip Collins had power and Joe "Ducky" Medwick could really hit. Other than that, they had guys who scratched and clawed their way to runs. Frankie Frisch, the "Fordham Flash," was their player/manager, and they had scrappy infielders Pepper Martin and Leo Durocher. They were so loud and energetic that they came to be known as the Gashouse Gang.

Frisch started Dizzy Dean in Game 1 and Cochrane gave the ball to General Crowder, who had started two games for the Senators in the 1933 World Series.

We played that game like a team that had never been there. Our infielders committed five errors. They beat us 8–3. Medwick had four hits and hit a home run and Dizzy pitched the whole game.

We had Schoolboy Rowe going for us in the second game. Nobody ever called him Lynwood—it was always Schoolboy. As a youngster in Arkansas, he pitched for an adult team in town, and was known as Schoolboy ever since.

Schoolie pitched all 12 innings for us in Game 2 and we won 3–2 to tie up the Series. Gee Walker singled in the tying run for us in the ninth, but he never should have gotten the chance to drive in that run. Earlier in his turn at bat, he had hit a pop foul that fell in between Bill Delancey, the catcher, and Collins, the first baseman. Goose singled home Gehringer for the winning run in the twelfth.

The Series moved to St. Louis and they won Game 3, 4–1, when Martin had a big game at the plate and Paul Dean got the complete game win for them.

We tied up the Series again by winning Game 4, 10–4. I went all the way for the win and gave up 10 hits. Rogell knocked in four runs and Greenberg drove home three.

That game remains memorable not for anything I did on the mound but for what I still consider to be the stupidest move ever made by a manager. For some reason none of us could understand, Frisch let Dizzy Dean talk him into using him as a pinch-runner. Imagine that, putting his ace pitcher in to pinch run at first base.

Whoever was at the plate at the time hit a grounder to Gehringer; right off the bat you knew it was a double-play ball. Rogell came across second base and threw to first for what looked like an easy double play. Dizzy went into second base standing up, instead of sliding. Rogell's throw hit him right in the forehead. Thank God it grazed off his cap's bill before hitting him. Still, it hit him hard enough to knock him out. He went down just like someone shot him. The stands went dead silent. We all went over there to see what was wrong with him. We feared the worst. When you think about it, a ball thrown at full speed, with the runner right on top of him, well, it's a good thing it grazed his cap bill. That cap bill might have saved his life. He was quiet on the ground, blinking his eyes. We finally got him on his feet and they took him to the hospital.

The next day, the St. Louis paper said that the doctors had X-rayed Dean's head and found nothing. That became a famous line for years.

We took our first lead in the Series, three games to two, by winning Game 5, 3–1. Tommy Bridges, pitching on one day of rest after going four innings in a Game 3 loss, had his best stuff this time. They had trouble hitting his curveball and he didn't need any help from the bullpen. Gehringer's home run was the big hit for us.

On the very next day after getting drilled on the forehead by Rogell's throw, Dizzy Dean started and went eight innings for St. Louis and took the loss.

It was Paul Dean's turn in Game 6, while we sent Schoolboy to the mound. They both pitched pretty well and neither one of them needed any help from the bullpen. Paul Dean singled in the winning run for a 4–3 Cardinals victory that evened the Series and necessitated a Game 7.

There never should have been a Game 7. The Cardinals had Brick Owens, the third-base umpire in Game 6, to thank for pushing the Series to the limit.

Brick Owens was not a good umpire. He was getting along in years at that point and he was stubborn as hell. The photographers proved that he blew a pivotal call late in Game 6. The picture that ran in the papers in Detroit the next day said it all.

The picture shows Mickey Cochrane sliding into third base with one leg folded up under him and the other foot touching the bag. Pepper Martin has his glove hand stretched out, waiting for the ball. The ball is about four feet away from his glove and Brick Owens is there with his thumb up in the air, signaling an out. He wasn't in position to make the call, and he just blew it.

We would have had the bases loaded with nobody out if the correct call had been made, and I believe to this day that we would have broken the game open and won the World Series that afternoon.

Anyway, that's neither here nor there because Cochrane was called out at third and there is nothing anybody can do about that now. The Series went to seven games.

I never have seen an entire city await anything with such an obsession as Detroit waited for Game 7 of that Series. World Series tickets were sold on a game-by-game basis in those days, and the streets around what was then called Navin Field (later it became Briggs Stadium, then Tiger Stadium) were packed with people trying to get tickets. The line snaked all around the stadium. They brought their dinners and their breakfasts and some people even brought their beds to sleep on through the night. It was some scene.

When they finally were allowed in the stadium for Game 7, they had their lunches with them, packed with apples and oranges, and some of them had bottled drinks. There were no canned drinks in those days, just bottles of soda and beer.

That game turned out to be one of the wildest in the history of the World Series. It was talked about and written about for years.

I started for us and Dizzy got the start for the Cardinals. We were good friends. We talked a little before the game and shook hands.

It was a scoreless game going into the third inning and they loaded the bases against me with two outs. Frisch was at the plate and the count was full. He fouled off three or four pitches. I threw another one inside, on his fists, and he pulled it toward Hank Greenberg at first base. It was a deceptive ball. It looked as if he had hit it harder than he actually did, and it fooled Hank. Hank jumped just a little bit too soon. He didn't time it quite right. It tipped his glove and the ball went into right field. Naturally, with the count full and two men out, the runners were sprinting with the pitch.

Pete Fox was playing right field for us and he came in to field the ball, which had rolled into a concrete drain that ran along the stands. Pete had his metal spikes on and slipped on the concrete, accidentally kicking the ball. It rolled down that drain and ended up in front of the Cardinal dugout by the time Cochrane fielded it. Three runs scored and Mickey took me out of the game and brought in Schoolboy to relieve. Then he brought in Chief Hogsett and it wasn't until he brought in Tommy Bridges that we got out of the inning. The Cardinals had seven runs in that inning.

The stands were filled and the people were so disappointed. They knew right then that it was over.

The suspense might have been over, but the most memorable incident from that game, the one that was talked about for decades, hadn't yet happened.

In the eighth inning of that game, Ducky Medwick hit one off the wall in center field for a triple. Medwick slid into third base with his spikes flying high. He spiked our third baseman, Marv Owen, and cut his uniform. Owen thought he did it on purpose, so they got into a scuffle. Owen took the ball and I guess tried to ram the ball down Medwicks's throat. Nobody was hurt, which was a good thing for Owen. Medwick was a real muscle man and he could have killed Owen. Marvin Owen was a tall, skinny kid, an easygoing, nice boy.

When it was time for Medwick to go back out to left field, the fans, who hadn't had much cause to make noise all afternoon, unloaded all their frustrations on Medwick. And that's not all they unloaded. They reached into their lunch bags and rifled oranges and apples toward him. They even tossed some soda and beer bottles in his direction. They threw whatever they could get their hands on onto left field.

Ty Tyson, the public address announcer, pleaded with the people to quit throwing things onto the field. He said that if they didn't stop what they were doing, the Tigers were going to have to forfeit the game.

The commissioner of baseball, Judge Landis—there was no mistaking him, with his wild white hair flopping all over the place—walked out to shortstop and called Medwick in from left field.

Seeking to restore order and realizing that the Cardinals had the game well in hand, Judge Landis decided to remove Medwick from the game. Medwick got upset all over again, but there was nothing he could do but leave the game, so he did.

They beat us, 11–0.

I was so disappointed with how the game went that I left the ballpark after seven innings. Through a clubhouse boy, I sent word to Mildred, who was in the stands, that I was going home without waiting for the game to end. I was out of the game and couldn't go back in, anyway. I was so exhausted from the long grind I just wanted to go home and beat the madhouse crowd out of there. I listened to the last two innings on the radio and nobody even noticed that I had left early.

We were all back the next day, cleaning out our lockers and saying our good-byes.

It's kind of a hard thing for people to believe or understand, but when you go through a long season and a pennant drive, reaching the World Series is almost a letdown as far as your intensity goes.

We played about 30 exhibitions during the spring. Then during the season, on our "off" day, Monday, we would go to Grand Rapids or Battle Creek and play an exhibition game. That was how the ballclub would generate a little extra money in those days, with exhibition games. We hardly had any days off. We would play 154 regular season games. We would play each of the other seven teams in our league 22 times. Then, when you're in a pennant race, it's pushing and pushing and pushing to win, every day, every day, every day. You're operating at a high level of intensity all the time. The pitchers, the hitters, the infielders, the outfielders, everybody is playing at such a high level of intensity and as soon as that game is over you are concentrating on the next one. And you do that for six months and something like 200 ballgames.

When you come to the end in late September and you look out and you have won the league and you're in the World Series, there is a real letdown and everybody relaxes. When it's your first time, getting to the World Series is the big thing.

You go into the World Series and for the people who root for the team, it's a big, exciting deal. I'm not saying it isn't fun to be there, but we had even *more* excitement in the drive for the pennant. We knew in the World Series that the most we could go was seven more games, and then, thank God, the season is over.

By that point, you're exhausted, physically and mentally. Guys would lose weight during the pennant drive because we were playing in the hot afternoon sun every day. Playing in Washington, St. Louis, Philadelphia, in the hot sun.

As far as losing it, well, we just lost the game and that was that. Frisch coming up with the bases loaded and two outs and getting that hit was the crux of it as far as I was concerned. They blew it open and the next day we all said the hell with it, we lost and now we're going home.

The truth is, though, the way Dizzy was throwing that day we weren't going to score any runs off him even if we had played for 20 innings. He was on and when he was right, nobody was better. He was right that day.

He had a great sinkerball and great control. He knew what he was doing out there, really knew how to pitch. If he found out a spot to get you out on, he could hit it just about every time when he needed to hit it. When he got into some trouble, he could hit that spot. Otherwise, he would just throw it down the middle and let you hit it. He'd challenge you. But like all good pitchers, he didn't pitch to your weak spot until he got in trouble.

A few years later, Dizzy was pitching in the All-Star Game and Earl Averill hit a line drive back at him and broke his pitching toe. Dizzy was on crutches for a week or 10 days. He was with the Cubs at the time and their doctor told him not to pitch until his toe healed. He didn't listen and returned to pitching too soon. He couldn't push off the rubber with his foot in a normal way and to compensate he started pitching with just his arm and not his body. That adjustment led to arm troubles and he wasn't the same pitcher after that.

But there was nothing wrong with either his arm or his mechanics in that memorable Game 7. Dizzy was right. He and Paul won 'em all. For us, our big thrill was in getting there. Once we had done that, however, getting back wouldn't be enough. We had to get back and win it. That was what was on our minds when we reported for spring training for our second season under Mickey Cochrane. From day one of the next spring, we set out to win the World Series.

/

Chapter 7

Goose Called It

Goose Goslin, a farm boy from South Jersey, came to us from the Senators before the 1934 season, bringing us more than the left-handed power hitter we needed to complement Hank Greenberg. He was always one to clown around and keep the players loose. He was some character, a really great guy. He was just happy-go-lucky, always laughing and joking and pulling pranks. He wasn't married and I guess you could say he was a happy bachelor. We used to have him out to the house with his girlfriend and he would always ask Mildred to make him onion sandwiches on Jewish rye bread. He washed them down with Stroh's beer. The four of us would play bridge; Goose was an accomplished bridge player.

Goose and Ernie Lombardi waged an ongoing feud over the years about who had the bigger nose. Lombardi, a catcher for the Reds, was known to all of us as "The Schnoz." Lombardi was a big, tall man who must have weighed 230, 240 pounds. He had an arm on him and he had an unorthodox throwing style for a catcher. He didn't throw over the top like most catchers. He was closer to sidearm, maybe more like three-quarters. And did he ever have a great, big nose. But Goose had quite a beak as well.

Goose Goslin taking a practice swing. *Photo courtesy of the Associated Press.*

"Schnoz, you're the only guy I know who can smoke a cigar in the shower," Goose would tell Lombardi, meaning that his nose was longer than any cigar and would keep it dry.

They never stopped going at each other about the size of their noses. Which guy was right? They both were. Both of them could get by on one breath a day.

We trained in Lakeland, Florida, and the Reds trained in Tampa. Every year on our way north at the end of camp we would play the Reds. We would play exhibitions with the Reds all the way up in one town after another. We played in every little town in North Carolina and we played in Atlanta. We always ended up in Cincinnati to play against the Reds on a Saturday and Sunday. Then we would take the train to Detroit on Monday morning and always opened the season on a Tuesday.

One spring, in our final exhibition in Cincinnati on a Sunday, Goose came up to the plate for the second time. Goose would swing so hard that he would swing himself completely around and make a complete circle. We had a man on first base. Goose took one of his big swings, turned completely around as usual, and Lombardi, who was catching, tried to throw out the runner stealing second. Lombardi went to throw the ball and his hand went right into Goslin's face, hit him right under the left eye, and pushed his nose all the way over and pretty near shattered it. Goose dropped onto the ground, knocked out. He was bleeding like a stuck hog. Blood ran out of his mouth and flowed from his nose.

Lombardi, a big, easygoing guy, looked down at Goose and said what were among the funniest words any of us ever heard uttered on a baseball field.

"That settles it," Lombardi said, staring at the injured man. "You've got the bigger nose. You've got such a damn big nose I can't even throw to second base. You can't get that nose out of the way."

Goose went to the hospital to get his nose set, and the two men remained close friends.

Goose was always regaling us with tales of pranks he had pulled in years past. Once he told us the story of the day he went to the picture show with Oscar Melillo, a second baseman for the Senators who was scared to death of birds, rabbits, and any number of other animals. Whenever he came to bat, Mickey Cochrane would yell, "Hey Oscar, look out, there's a snake at your feet," or "Look out for that jackrabbit, Oscar."

Anyway, Goose told us that when they went to the theater in Orlando, there was a little kitten outside. Goose let Melillo walk ahead, scooped the kitten into his arms, and carried it inside with him. The show had already started when Goose took the cat and threw it on Melillo's back.

"Get this thing off of me! Get this thing off of me!" he screamed as he rolled around the floor.

On came the lights and off went the show. The kitten had scurried away by then, and here's this grown man rolling around on the floor, screaming. He looked around and couldn't find Goose anywhere. They came in to escort him out of there and he said, "Wait, you better get Goose Goslin, too. He came here with me."

They didn't know what the hell he was talking about. They thought he was a crazy man. Here he was rolling around on the floor one minute, babbling about a goose the next.

That was Goose. Always pulling a prank, forever laughing and joking. Yet when I think about Goose, he couldn't have been more serious than in the moment that first comes to mind.

After the disappointment of losing the 1934 World Series to the Cardinals in the seventh game, we were determined to win it all in 1935. And win it all we did, thanks in large part to Goose Goslin.

This time we faced the Cubs, and they had a distinctly different personality from the Gashouse Gang. The Cubs packed their dugout with gentlemen. Gabby Hartnett was their catcher, quite a gentleman and a great ballplayer. He was the National League MVP that year. Lon Warneke, the pitcher who dominated us that October, was one of the nicest guys you ever wanted to meet. He was just a big, old Arkansas hillbilly. Bill Lee was the top pitcher in the league that year. He was a nice-looking young man, big and strong and another real gentleman. Charlie Root was another nice guy. Same goes for Billy Herman, their second baseman.

Sportswriters are fond of writing about how much athletes have changed, often not for the better. That might be true, but they haven't changed as much as sportswriters.

One man wrote for the *Detroit Free Press* under the name, "Iffy the Dopester." An excerpt from one of his 1935 columns:

> "I pick Cleveland to win the flag this year," said Connie Mack this spring.
>
> "Why Cleveland?" Old Iffy demanded, tearing at his whiskers with considerable rage, for him, for he had picked the Tigers to repeat.
>
> "Well," said Old Rain-in-the-Face Cornelius, "there's Trosky for one thing. He is a great natural slugger and he will be the rightful successor of Babe Ruth."
>
> That was in the spring, tra la, O, my hearties, and this is August. If you will search the American League batting averages you will find Trosky hitting .274 among the routine batsmen.
>
> And Homer Hank, the Big Greenberg Boy, has taken the place vacated by the passing of the belching, belting Bambino—not Trosky.
>
> But this need not be any reflection on the keen Connie. Usually the judgments of the McGillicuddy are true and righteous altogether.

We had our hands full with the Cubs, especially since Greenberg broke his wrist late in the second game and was out for the rest of the Series. Greenberg had such a great year that he was voted American League MVP in 1935.

The Cubs were the hottest team in baseball at the end of the year. They spent most of the season in third place, behind the Cardinals and the Giants, then raced past both of those teams by winning 21 straight games in September.

We opened the Series just as we had the previous year, with fingers made of butter. We committed three errors and lost 3–0. Warneke pitched a four-hit shutout.

Greenberg's two-run home run was the highlight of our 8–3, Game 2 victory; his wrist injury was the lowlight.

We went to Chicago with the Series even, and I faced Bill Lee in Game 3. We both were lifted for pinch-hitters in a tight ballgame that we won, 6–5, when Jo Jo White drove Marv Owen home on a single in the 11th inning.

General Crowder pitched a 2–1 victory in Game 4 to put us ahead in the Series, three games to one. We tried to clinch it in Chicago, but Warneke, making his third appearance of the Series, shut us out for six innings before leaving the game with a sore shoulder. Lee retired Flea Clifton with two outs and runners on second and third in the ninth to save their 3–1 win, which sent the Series back to Detroit.

Our fans, who had been let down the year before, were on edge as we headed into the ninth inning of Game 6 with the score tied, 3–3.

I was sitting on the dugout steps at the start of our half of the ninth and Goose was sitting beside me. He was the fourth hitter due up that inning. He turned to me and said something I'll never forget.

"I've got a hunch," Goose said. "I'm going to be up there with the winning run on base and we're going to win this ballgame.

I've just got a feeling in my bones I'm going to be up there with the winning run on base and I'm going to drive him in."

The Goose wasn't joking this time. It played out exactly that way.

Mickey Cochrane got on base, took second on Charlie Gehringer's hard-hit one-hopper to first, and was standing there waiting to be driven in with the winning run when Goose came to the plate to face Larry French, the left-hander who went the whole way for them that day. Goose fouled off the first pitch, then jumped on the second one and lined it into right field, over the reach of leaping Billy Herman, to score Cochrane from second. We won 4–3, giving Detroit's beloved Tigers their first World Series title.

The record-breaking Navin Field crowd of 48,420 went crazy. Goose ran right through everybody who had stormed the field and I ran toward him. He threw his arms around me and started hollering, "What'd I tell ya? What'd I tell ya? What'd I tell ya?"

It was the culmination of a great two-year run. It was fitting that it was Cochrane who scored the winning run because he was our leader. It was also fitting that Goose played a part. We became a different team the moment those two came to us before the 1934 season. They both later made it to the Hall of Fame, along with Greenberg and Gehringer.

When you win it all, you have reason to celebrate—you have to go through so much just to get there. We had gotten off to a slow start and were in sixth place in May. But once we got hot, we stayed hot.

When you win the World Series, you think back to so many things. I thought back to the Fourth of July, when we were in St. Louis to play the Browns. The temperature was 115° and I pitched nine innings. I changed my uniform three times. I lost 11 pounds pitching that ballgame, even though I was in perfect shape before it started. It was the first game of a doubleheader and St. Louis used about five pitchers. I took salt tablets to keep from getting dehydrated and had just a swallow of water. You can't drink too much water or you get cramps. When it was over, I got a stool, sat down in the shower, and just let that water run over me for about an hour to cool me down. I slept pretty well that night.

And I slept pretty well the night we won the World Series, too, which is more than I can say for most of the city.

In the clubhouse, we hugged each other and were all so happy, but we weren't spraying champagne around or even drinking it. That tradition didn't start until long after I was done playing. Most of us just wanted to get home and stay away from the people. They were going so crazy that if they had seen one of us, they would have torn our clothes off.

The town went crazy, absolutely crazy. They upset streetcars, turned them right over. The people were not trying to be destructive, but they just went wild and in their enthusiasm they were destructive. There wasn't any vandalism, wasn't any breaking into windows and looting or any of that sort of thing, but they raised hell in the streets all night long. The impromptu parade stretched well into the morning. The police estimated the crowd in the streets at a half million people, a bigger celebration than Armistice Day in 1918.

Later, some fan started a movement creating a write-in campaign to make Mickey Cochrane a city councilman. Those people were mad for Mickey Cochrane.

My wife, Mildred, and I returned to our apartment on Chicago Boulevard, ready to enjoy a quiet evening alone together, when the phone rang. It was Harvey Frauhoff, the head of Frauhoff Trailers; Mildred and I were good friends with him and his wife. He invited us to join them at the Detroit Athletic Club as his guest, and we accepted.

In those days, they always had entertainers at the clubs and on this particular night they had a little blond gal from the South named Dinah Shore. She was very well known, and she put on a wonderful show that night.

The chef made a Detroit Tiger out of ice and they wheeled that ice tiger in front of our table while the band played "Hold That Tiger." I was the only player there, and it was a nice, quiet evening for us.

Each of us players received a record World Series share of $6,831.88. I think my salary was $12,000 that year. Mr. Navin was in the clubhouse afterward along with Judge Landis and Will Harridge, president of the American League.

That would be the last I would see of Mr. Navin. Mildred and I went home to Kansas for Thanksgiving; a sad telegram was waiting for us when we arrived. Mr. Navin had passed away. He had fallen off a horse. We didn't even stay all night with my dad and mom. We turned right around and drove all the way back to Detroit for the funeral. Super highways had not been built yet, so it took 24 hours to drive from Norcatur to Detroit.

Mr. Navin had been there for us once in a time of need. He was like a second dad to a lot of the players and he really came through for Mildred and me when we needed help at the beginning of the 1934 season.

Mildred had driven up from spring training to Poplar Bluff, Missouri, to visit her brother. From there she drove on to Chicago and met us for Opening Day. Mildred had everything we owned in that car except for a few changes of clothes and a shaving kit that I had in a bag with me. I gave her everything else I had brought to spring training and she drove back to Detroit while I went with the team to Cleveland to play on Friday, Saturday, and Sunday. We took the train back to the Fort Street Station in Detroit on Sunday night.

Five or six thousand fans were there to greet us for the start of the season. The wives were allowed to wait in a special, private area. We all went over to greet our wives and everyone was very happy except Mildred. When she came toward me she was crying. I thought some family member might have died.

"What's the matter honey?" I asked.

"We were robbed," she said, sobbing. "Our car was broken into and they stole everything we have. They took every single piece of clothing we own."

She told me how it happened. She had gone out to Grosse Pointe, a nice section of Detroit, to visit Ralph Baker and his wife. Baker was an assistant prosecutor for the city of Detroit. Mildred left our car, locked, in front of their house and the three of them went out to dinner. When they came back to the house around 9:00, Baker convinced Mildred to spend the night at their house; so, they went out to the car to get her overnight bag. When they walked outside, they discovered that all of the windows had been smashed, the trunk had been broken into, and the entire car was cleaned out. Mildred didn't have anything but the clothes on her back.

I went down to the park on Monday, the day before our home opener, driving our smashed-up car. I was told Mr. Navin wanted to see me. I thought, "Oh boy. We have $64 to our name and not a stitch of clothing, and he's calling me in to tell me I'm being released and we don't even have enough money to get out of town."

The incident had been reported in the papers, in part because it happened right in front of an assistant district attorney's house. "I understand you had some hard luck," Mr. Navin said to me. "I read in the papers you were robbed. Did they get everything?"

"They got everything."

"Do you have money?" he asked.

"I have $64."

"Did they get your clothes?" he asked.

"They got every piece of clothing we have."

"Well, we're going out on the road next week and you're going to have to have some clothes and your wife is going to have to have some clothes," he said. He walked out of the room and came back a few minutes later with a check for $500. Mildred bought enough clothes to get by and I went down and bought a suit for $19.95, which came with two pairs of pants.

You don't forget kindness like that.

Nobody would ever have guessed that Mr. Briggs would outlive Mr. Navin, but he did. Mr. Briggs, as per their agreement, inherited Mr. Navin's portion of the team. Navin Field became Briggs Stadium and the relationship between the players and the owner became a little frostier.

We would have won more than just the one World Series if Mr. Briggs had left Cochrane alone to run the team. But he always wanted to put his stamp on it. He was a big fan and he thought he knew how to run the team better than Cochrane did.

Nevertheless, we won the World Series. Nobody can take that away from us.

Chapter 8

Home-Baked
Humble Pie

During those World Series years in Detroit, the whole town treated us like kings. It had been so long since the Tigers played in a World Series that the people were eager to show us how much they appreciated what we had accomplished. They were forever asking for our autographs and always wanted to take us out to dinner or entertain us at their expense. People were tripping all over each other to do things for us. We were big shots, all right. When you're young and you get treated like that all year long, if you're not careful to keep your feet on the ground, you start to think that you're pretty darned important.

And then you go home again.

Mildred and I decided to go home to visit our folks in Norcatur and Manhattan, Kansas, after the 1934 World Series. Because I pitched for the Tigers, I had a special arrangement with a local Pontiac dealer. When the brand-new models came out at the end of the season, all I had to pay was $100 to have the use of a brand-new car for a year. We drove that car to my little home-town of about 500 people.

"Let's sneak into town in the evening so the band won't be out there to greet us," I said to Mildred with a smile on my face. "We're going back home, so let's just act like normal people. Let's not act like the big shots we really are now." We arrived and were happy to discover that there was no band there to greet us in my cowboy hometown.

The next morning I told my mom and Mildred that I was going uptown to see my dad, who was the town's mail carrier, and several other old friends. The town was only two blocks long. Dr. Pool, the town dentist, was right next door to Dr. Smith. They were two of the sharper men in town. The general store, run by a man by the name of Jake Keener, was next to that. I came out of Dr. Smith's office and was going in to see Jake Keener in the general store when I ran into John Holland, who had come to pick up his mail.

The Holland family has been in Norcatur since the birth of our little town. John Holland was an older gentleman, about 60 I guess, and I was 24 at the time. My mother had done some baby-sitting for the Hollands and John had known me since the day I was born.

Ever mindful of keeping it low-key, I stuck my hand out to shake and said, "John, how are you?"

He returned my handshake and said, "Oh, Elden, how are you?"

"Just fine," I said. "How've you been, anyway? You getting along all right? You feel good?"

"Oh, yes, I feel pretty good," he said.

We were about to go our separate ways when he stopped, cocked his head to the side a little, squinted his eyes, and served me a hefty slice of home-baked humble pie by way of a question I'll never forget: "Say, Elden, where the hell have you been any-way? I haven't seen you all summer." He hadn't heard a thing about my "big-time" baseball career.

All I ever had to do to keep from getting a big head was go back home to Norcatur, where, instead of being a baseball star, I was the mail carrier's son, first, foremost, and always.

I finally was honored by my hometown when they dedicated a park to me, but that wasn't until almost the 21st century. Not everyone followed baseball back in 1934. There was no television, of course, so baseball didn't get near the exposure it does today. And my folks were proud of me for making it to the major leagues, but it's not like they had reason to grow big heads over it, either.

Back when I was playing baseball, my dad and Clint Carper, a fellow who owned a grocery store where I worked part-time for a spell, would drive about 40 miles away to the little town of Western, Nebraska, sandhill country, to go fishing. They would hop into his car as soon as Dad finished his mail route and spend the night in a campground. It was very sparsely settled territory, with maybe one farm every 10 or 12 miles.

Carper had an old Motorola radio fastened on the steering wheel of his car and was forever tuning it as he drove along. He would hit one bump in the road and it would shake the wires loose. I was pitching a ballgame in Chicago once and my dad and Carper were driving along, listening to the game. The radio signal went out on them during the third or fourth inning and they were all upset. They fiddled and fiddled with the wires but just couldn't pick up the signal again. Finally, they came to a filling station way out in the country. They noticed a little aerial on top of the building. They pulled in there and my dad jumped out of the car and ran inside to see if they had the ballgame on the radio. The young country boy (wearing overalls) who was running the filling station came outside. Clint asked him how the ballgame was coming along.

"What ballgame is that?" the boy asked.

"There's a baseball game being played in Chicago and I see you have that aerial and I thought maybe you were listening to the ballgame," Clint said.

"Oh, that radio hasn't worked in years," he said, pointing to an old Atwater radio. "It went on the bum and I never did get it fixed."

"Well, the reason I'm asking is that fellow who ran in there, his name is Fred Auker. His son is Elden Auker," Clint said.

The boy returned a blank stare.

"Elden Auker. He's a pitcher for the Detroit Tigers," Clint persisted. "Did you ever hear of Elden Auker?"

"No," the boy said.

"He's pitching for the Detroit Tigers right now against the White Sox and we were listening on the radio and our radio. . . . "

"Oh, baseball," the boy said, interrupting. "The Tigers and the White Sox. I don't know much about baseball."

"You never heard of Elden Auker?" Clint asked again.

"No, I can't say that I have," the boy replied. "I heard of Babe Ruth."

As a child, my own knowledge of baseball players wasn't much better than that of the country boy who ran that filling station. I too had heard of Babe Ruth, but that was about it.

I graduated from high school in 1928; it wasn't until my senior year that we had a radio and they weren't broadcasting much baseball back then. The only way you could follow baseball was in the papers. Kansas City was the closest big town and *The Kansas City Star* came in on the train a day late. You could read about baseball in the *Star*, although I never did. I was working and going to school and had other things on my mind besides following baseball.

We kids were always throwing a baseball or a football around, always playing catch, but as far as getting a group of kids together to play a baseball game? Never. We didn't have a high school baseball team because I was the only kid at school who played, so I joined a town team for adults.

As kids we would go for a swim or hunt for squirrels and rabbits and pheasants. When I turned 12 years old, my dad gave me a 410-gauge shotgun, and that was a big deal to me. I still have that shotgun, and it still shoots. Ours was a western town and every household had a gun, if not three or four. All the kids in town had guns and we all knew how to handle them. It never even occurred to us that you could use a gun to injure somebody. Those guns were for hunting, and hunt we did.

We would go out in a group of three or four and scare up jackrabbits. Cottontail rabbits are the little bunnies you see hopping around; a jackrabbit's a bigger rabbit with longer ears. Kansas was covered with them. Driving at night on the highway you'd run into half a dozen of them going someplace together. The men in town used to have roundups to get rid of them because they ate up the crops. Jackrabbits are good eatin', and so are squirrels. Don't ever let anybody tell you otherwise unless you've tried them yourself. Rabbit is excellent meat. It tastes like—you guessed it—chicken, only better.

We used to shoot a lot of crows, too, and those things were hard to kill. They're smart. You can walk out onto a field with no gun and those crows will sit on a post right next to you, not paying you any mind. But you walk out there with a gun in your hand and you can't find a crow within 10 miles of you. Those suckers know when you've got a gun. You would have to hide when you wanted to shoot a crow. We would shoot them in the evening when they came in to roost.

The area was prairie land, good for raising cattle and growing wheat. The ground was as hard as a rock. The grass looked like it was on the verge of death one day, and then it would rain and the grass would be just as green as can be. There was no lumber because there were hardly any trees, other than fruit trees such as the apricot, apple, and peach trees we had in our yard.

Because of the shortage of trees, when the area was first settled they built houses out of grass. They cut bricks of sod and put the grass side on the outside of the house. They whitewashed it on the inside and made plaster with the inside-out soil. My mother was born in a "soddy," and lived to ride in a jet aircraft.

My mother's father was a homesteader. President Grant gave 640 acres to anyone who would go west to farm the land. My grandfather settled 12 miles from the Nebraska line, about 15 miles from the trail that was going west when the gold rush was on. As a child, I loved hearing stories of how he used to capture wild horses, break them, and take them up to the trail to sell them.

People used to come in from all over the southwest to harvest the Kansas wheat. Today, farmers have equipment that can do all that.

There used to be a saloon in town, but that shut down. Prohibition was enacted when I was a kid and the town became dry. We had tornadoes and cyclones and prairie fires, but we didn't have a saloon.

The advantage of growing up in a small town, other than keeping you levelheaded when you start to thinking you're a big shot, is that everybody knows everybody. Everyone in town knew me by the time I was six weeks old. When he first started the mail route my father used horses—two for each half of the route. By the time I was born, he used the horses to pull a wagon in the winter but covered the route by motorcycle when the weather was nicer. When I was six weeks old, my mother got on behind him with me in her arms and he took us around his route and introduced me to all the folks. He made $60 a month and had to cover the horse expenses out of his own pocket.

News from the outside world was slow to come to Norcatur, but communication within the town never stalled, thanks to the Craig family. Our telephone was a box on the wall with a ringer on it. To make a call you would call what was known as "central." The Craig family operated every aspect of it: they owned the franchise, installed the equipment, took care of the maintenance, and operated the switchboard. Each family shared a party line with three or four others. Each ring was different so everyone would

Elden Auker shares a quiet moment at the ballpark with his father, Fred. *Photo from the personal collection of Elden Auker.*

know who the call was for. My aunt and uncle, for example, might have had a "two-long-rings" signal. Somebody else might have one long ring and one short one. I would listen to my mother talk to the operator: "I'm fine, thank you, Sheila. Would you ring Coral for me, please?"

Norcatur hadn't changed a great deal when Mildred and I came back for our visit after the '34 World Series. By not giving us the celebrity treatment we received in Detroit, the town folk saw to it that *we* didn't change, either.

After our nice visit to my hometown, we drove over to Manhattan, where Mildred's folks were living. Mildred's grandfather lived with them; he was about 90 years old at the time. Mildred wanted me to meet her grandfather, who, like mine, was a homesteader.

Grandpa Purcell looked just like a Kentucky colonel, with his white beard and long, white hair. He had come from Purcellsville,

Virginia, and settled in Kansas after receiving a homestead grant. When Mildred's father was six months old, Grandpa Purcell headed west in a covered wagon with his wife, his two daughters, and his infant son. He became one of the pillars of the community in Chase, Kansas.

Mildred introduced us and we sat down and had a nice chat.

"Do you own any land?" he asked me, measuring what sort of provider I'd be for his granddaughter, I suppose.

"No, I really don't," I told him.

"You were born in Norcatur, were you?" he asked.

"Yes, sir, I was."

"What does your dad do?" he asked.

I told him, and he then asked if I had a job.

"Yes, I do," I said. "I play baseball."

He was certain I had misunderstood him. "No, I mean how do you make your living?" he asked.

"Playing professional baseball," I said.

If someone had told me that I had a third eye on my forehead it wouldn't have come as a surprise at that moment, since Grandpa Purcell was looking at me as if I were a man from Mars.

"I don't understand you," he said. "They pay you to play baseball?"

"Yes, sir, that's right," I said.

"Well, who pays you?"

"The Detroit Tigers," I replied.

"Where do *they* get the money to pay you?"

"The people who come to see us pay to get into the games," I said.

This was all news to him. He was more in the dark about baseball players than that country boy at the filling station.

I tried to explain to him that there was an American League and a National League. I told him what cities had teams in each league and that we had crowds of 30,000 people that came to see us play in Detroit. He never could visualize it.

"I used to play baseball," he said. "And we even used to have people come out to watch us play, but they sure never paid to see us."

While he tried to absorb the strange concept of professional baseball, he asked if I ever took a drink. I told him I enjoyed a beer every now and then.

"Come with me," he said.

He took me back to what was called a cooling house. Back in those days, they didn't have refrigerators. To keep things cool, they had deep wells of water and would pump that water through a tank; the water was flowing all the time. He reached down into it, pulled out a little bottle of bourbon, and told me to have a drink with him, which I took as a sign that I had passed the test and gained his acceptance.

"A little bourbon never hurt anybody," he said.

Just because I had the silliest, most unimportant means of making a living the man had ever heard of, that didn't mean I wasn't worthy of sharing a glass of bourbon with him. And right he was—a little bourbon didn't hurt me.

Imagine how surprised Grandpa Purcell would have been to learn that my little hometown would someday dedicate a park in my name. It happened on May 27, 2000. Jim Nelson, whose parents used to go on fishing trips in Texas with my folks, dedicated the land to the city with the stipulation that it had to be used for a park in the middle of town. Mildred and I had last been home in 1983 for my mother's funeral.

Guess what? A band was there to greet us this time. The small town band played *The Star Spangled Banner* as the flag was raised. It was a nice, memorable day.

The town has changed some, of course. Everything changes. It has gotten smaller, shrinking from about 500 people when I was a boy to about 350 now. Sons inherit farms from their fathers and have to give them up because they can't afford the inheritance tax.

But a lot of people who once moved away for better jobs are now returning to Norcatur for their retirement years. It makes sense. Clocks tick quietly and slowly there. It's a humble town that makes sure all of its residents stay that way too.

Chapter 9

Big Six and
Changing Times

I scored 9 of our 10 points in one of my high school basketball tournament games. In those days, a 9-point game was enough to grab anybody's attention.

After the game, the referee asked me if I had any plans to attend college. I told him I planned to go to Nebraska, where I would take courses to prepare for medical school and play sports as well. I told him they had a job set up for me. There were no scholarships then.

"You're a Kansas boy and Kansas boys should go to college in Kansas," the referee told me. "We've got a job for you down here, too, so don't worry about that."

It sounded logical to me, although the referee wasn't completely unbiased. His name was Charlie Corseau, and he was the head varsity basketball and baseball coach at Kansas State University, in Manhattan, Kansas.

My job was to open up the on-campus drugstore in the morning, mop all the floors, and clean everything. At night, I mopped the floors again and locked it up. I was paid $1.00 for that. During the day, I was paid 25 cents an hour for working the soda fountain.

That might not sound like a lot of money, but in those days you could get breakfast for 15 cents, lunch for a quarter, and the best dinner in town for 35 cents.

I also had a job working at the school dances, if, that is, I was still able to walk after the football games.

I played football for Bo McMillin and basketball and baseball for Corseau. I earned All–Big Six honors in all three sports, which led to my collegiate nickname of Big Six. The sportswriters referred to me as that, but nobody in baseball ever did. At the time, there was a magazine called *College Humor*. That publication selected me for All-American honors in all three sports and said I was the first athlete so honored. They folded shortly after that, so I guess I was the *last* one so honored, too.

I was a football man. That was my sport, I guess maybe because I played for such a great coach. McMillin was a great psychologist. He really knew how to give us talks that fired us up. He was a lot like Mickey Cochrane in that way.

In many ways, the most memorable game I played for him was against Texas A&M. The game was in Dallas at the old Cotton Bowl, with those wooden stands. Greasy Neale was the coach for Texas, and they had a great football team.

In his 1947 book *Coach Phog Allen's Sports Stories*, the legendary Kansas basketball coach included his all-opponent teams from every season. His 1932 all-opponent team included Elden Auker (Kansas State), Andy Beck (Oklahoma), M. Collings (Missouri), Al Heitman (Iowa State), Jack Roadcap (Iowa State), and Andy Skradski (Kansas State).

McMillin, who had been married while still in college, and Neale played against each other as college athletes. McMillin's wife later died in childbirth, and the last game she ever saw her husband play in was against Greasy Neale. Because of these memories, this was a very emotional day for McMillin, and we all knew it.

Elden Auker during his football days at Kansas State. *Photo from the personal collection of Elden Auker.*

The Texas heat burned so hot on that September afternoon that you could barely catch your breath. The temperature must have been 115°. We had those long-sleeve uniforms made of heavy wool and heavy canvas pants. The collars of the jerseys wrapped around your neck and just about smothered you to death. Unlike us, the Texas team was dressed for the weather, wearing short sleeves.

The normal routine for McMillin was to bring us out onto the field to loosen up and then take us back into the locker room for a pep talk. By the time he was through talking, we believed we could take on the world.

He had been telling us all week about how important this game was to him. With tears in his eyes, he told us, "We're going on the field where my dear wife saw me play a football game for the last time before she died." Every time he thought or talked about it, he got tears in his eyes.

We were loosening up, kicking and punting and running through our signals before the game, when he called us together. Instead of taking us back into the locker room, this time he led us to the end of the field and had us all sit out in the hot sun. He stood in the middle of us and looked into the stands. Streams of tears started trickling down his face.

"I guess I don't have anything to say," he said, and then walked away and left us sitting there. That really tore our hearts out. We all sat there dumbfounded with tears in our eyes. We had all expected a big speech.

Finally, Hoxie Freeman, a great big tackle who was captain of the team, jumped to his feet and broke the silence.

"He didn't have anything to say, but by God I have something to say," Hoxie barked. "I don't know about the rest of you, but I'm going to be the best tackle on this field today. We're going to go out there and we're going to beat the hell out of them." We all hollered agreement, jumped up, and ran onto the field, determined to play the game of our lives.

Despite our determination, they beat us pretty soundly. It was so hot that we could barely breathe out there. Halfway through the first quarter, they had to carry Hoxie off the field. He was stricken by the heat and wasn't able to play another down.

Inspiration is a great aid in athletic competition, all right, but sometimes it's not enough to overcome talent and an opposing team that uses equipment suited to the conditions. This was one of those times.

After college I came close to signing a professional football contract with the Chicago Bears, but decided to play baseball instead. The Bears sent Bronko Nagurski, their great fullback, a bull of a man, and Bert Pearson, who had played at Kansas State, down to Manhattan to talk to me about coming to play for the Bears. I guess the main reason I chose baseball was because it allowed me to start playing and making money as soon as I graduated from college. If I had played football, I would have had to wait until the fall to start playing, and I wouldn't have had anything to do all summer.

In 1931 I was captain of the basketball team, and we had a shot at the Big Six title. We didn't win the title. Sadly, we finished second to Phog Allen's Kansas team.

I played guard in basketball. In those days, forwards did most of the shooting, while guards were defensive specialists. We played a zone defense and our responsibility was to stop anyone from getting close to the basket. It was a much more physical game than it is today.

Corseau had a rule that if an opponent went to the basket for a setup—that's what we called a layup back then—and came out of there standing up, the guard responsible was taken out of the game. If someone had the ball, they were fair game. As long as you were playing the ball and not the man, you could do whatever you wanted. If a guy was going in for a setup, you could take the ball out of his hands and knock him into the bleachers, and there would be no foul called.

We had a jump ball after every made basket and every held ball. As was the case in football, if you were taken out of a game, you couldn't go back in during that half.

All of the changes that have been made to basketball since then were designed to speed up the game. Now you see guys flying to the hoop all the time; in my day, they would never get airborne. They would stay on the ground. If they didn't, they would land on their heads and think twice about leaving the ground again.

Given all the substituting and all the specialization and shuttling of players in and out between every down, I would say the sport that's changed the most since my playing days is football. Because of the substitution rules back then, we would play both offense and defense. In most games we played all 60 minutes, barring a serious injury.

I think it's accurate to say that baseball has changed the least of the three sports I played. Not that baseball hasn't changed—it certainly has. But the changes have been subtler than in the other sports.

When I signed my first contract with the Tigers after graduating from Kansas State in 1932, Mr. Navin called me in and told me what he expected of me. "A game is nine innings long," he said. "We're paying you to pitch nine innings. So when you start a game, we expect you to finish it. That's the way we do things here." And that's what you expected of yourself, too. If you didn't finish the game, you felt as if you hadn't done your job. Now they make a big deal out of it if someone pitches a complete game.

The biggest, most frustrating, and most perplexing change in baseball involves the art of throwing inside. Moving hitters off the plate was part of the game in my day. Now, it's considered an act almost worthy of declaring war. It's ridiculous.

I was a pitcher. That plate was mine. Anyone who tried to take undue advantage—swinging too hard, really going after it, trying to show me up on the pitchers' mound—would have to pay for it. If a hitter got a couple of pretty good hits off me, I'd loosen him up. We used to say, "Let's see how he can hit laying down."

Of course, I'm not talking about trying to hit a batter in the head to hurt him. That wasn't the goal. I could have hit a guy in the head to hurt him any time I wanted to. All you had to do was throw the ball behind him, because the natural reaction is to back away from the ball. But if you throw at his head, he'll get his head out of the way. You can't hit him that way. So that wasn't what we tried to do.

If you throw the ball up and in, under the chin, you're not going to hit the guy in the head. You would always throw a fastball for a knockdown pitch, never a curveball. Or sometimes, if you wanted to hit a batter, you would stick it in his ribs, where he couldn't get out of the way. With some hitters, we just cut loose and knocked them flat on their backs. That was very effective against some of them.

In those days, the knockdown pitch was something that was just part of the game, part of pitching. If somebody was up at the plate with a bat in his hands, really wearing you out, backing him away from the plate was your only defense. We let them know when we thought they were being a little too brave. They were paid to hit and I was paid to get them out. They understood that.

Every once in a while, a hitter would get upset at being thrown at, but he would get over it. Joe Kuhel of the White Sox was so upset with me once that he socked me in the nose. I threw at him three times before I finally hit him. I glanced one off his head. But we shook hands the next day. Throwing at a hitter didn't put your friendship in jeopardy any more than him getting a few hits off of your pitching did.

There were some guys you didn't throw at because by doing so you would be waking them up, making them more dangerous than ever. Charlie Gehringer, Hank Greenberg, Babe Ruth, Ted Williams, you didn't throw at those guys.

Elden Auker and Joe Kuhel of the White Sox shake hands, refusing to let a physical altercation get the better of friendship. *Photo from the personal collection of Elden Auker.*

I'll tell you one thing that hasn't changed in baseball, despite what so many people who try to glorify our era at the expense of the modern players will tell you. We played for the money, too. To say we played for the love of the game is to perpetuate a myth. I liked baseball and it was certainly an enjoyable way to make a living, but the money is the only reason I played.

At first I was only playing so that I could save up enough money to pay for medical school. That's why I took anatomy, physiology, chemistry, and psychology courses at Kansas State. Then Mildred and I married in 1933, which added to my financial responsibility. And the depression made money so scarce that once I started earning such a good living at baseball, I couldn't afford to give up the paychecks. I never did get the chance to attend medical school.

It is true that once we were out on the field playing a game, money never entered our minds. All we cared about was winning. We weren't thinking about getting better statistics so that we could earn more money. Whether that aspect of it has changed, I really don't know. But I do know that we played baseball because somebody was willing to pay us for it.

The best change to the game, naturally, came when the Dodgers signed Jackie Robinson to a contract and opened the gates for athletes of all races. Before that, men of color were restricted to playing in the Negro leagues, a reality that gave baseball history the Kansas City Monarchs, a team formed of men who were part baseball players, part magicians.

Chapter 10

Town-Team Baseball and the Kansas City Monarchs

I stayed in Manhattan during the summer of 1931 to haul ice for an ice plant. I also played baseball for a "town team" called the Manhattan Travelers. Six of us from the Kansas State team joined up with a few players who had retired from the minor leagues. We played a 40-game schedule all over Kansas, Oklahoma, Colorado, and Nebraska. We were a pretty darn good team.

Our curiosity was running high before one particular game, and so was the excitement among the fans, who were eager to watch our famous opponents. The Kansas City Monarchs, the pride of the Negro Leagues, were in town. They had the legendary Satchel Paige pitching for them and were riding a 33-game winning streak when they made the 130-mile bus trip to play us.

The fans were so eager to watch us play that they built makeshift stands at a public park just for that game. I guess about 600 people came out to see us play the Monarchs that day.

We were all familiar with the legend of Satchel Paige. I had heard the story of how he had pitched five games in three days in a tournament in Denver, and had averaged 18 strikeouts a game.

We took infield practice first, in what amounted to a warm-up act before the main event. When the Monarchs took infield practice, we were treated to a show we wouldn't have thought possible.

They had a big catcher by the name of Big T. J. Young and a center fielder whose name I can't recall for certain. John McGraw once referred to Oscar Charleston as the greatest outfielder he ever saw, and I wouldn't be surprised if that was Oscar Charleston in center field that day. It's difficult to imagine anyone being a much better outfielder than this guy was. Young sat on his haunches behind home plate, the center fielder sat on his haunches in the outfield, and they played catch like that. The crowd was spellbound.

Their infielders were equally slick. The second baseman would take a throw from the shortstop, come across the bag, turn the double play, and never look at first base when he made the throw. The louder the crowd cheered, the crazier the Monarchs' antics became. They worked that ball around so fast while taking infield that it was hard to keep track of it. They could really play.

Paige pitched that ballgame for them. During the first few innings they were still doing crazy things to entertain the crowd. But once they saw that they were in for a tough fight and weren't scoring any runs, they got down to serious business.

Young hit a home run off me. There weren't any walls at the park and the ball just kept going and going and going. He had some kind of power, and he had a great throwing arm, too. There is no doubt in my mind that if blacks had been allowed to play in the majors, he would have been an All-Star catcher.

That was the only run they scored off me, and we won the game, 2–1.

Later in the summer, when it was thrashing season, I went back home to work the wheat fields. During that time I pitched for an all-salary town team out of Oxford, Nebraska. In order to maintain my amateur status, I played under the assumed name of Eddie Leroy. I pitched twice a week, on Wednesdays and Sundays. I was paid $75 for pitching a Sunday game and $50 for Wednesdays.

I also played against the Kansas City Monarchs with this team, this time in Arapahoe, Nebraska, where the county fair was taking place. I pitched against a guy by the name of Andy Cooper, a left-hander. I thought he was an even better pitcher than Satchel Paige. He had a better curveball than Paige. Even if he wasn't better, he

Long before Jackie Robinson broke baseball's color barrier, a black man who was every bit as much of a celebrity as Robinson, and every bit as tough, regularly worked out with the Tigers before games.

Joe Louis took groundballs at third base, shagged flyballs in the outfield, and took batting practice, usually with the pitchers. By all accounts, he did not hit a baseball as hard as he hit noses.

Joe Louis. Photo courtesy of the Associated Press.

"We all knew him and loved to have him around," Elden Auker said. "He was a good-looking guy, not quite as good-looking as Ali, and he always had that camel-hair coat on."

Louis won the heavyweight championship in 1935, the same year the Tigers won the World Series, the Lions won the NFL championship, and the Red Wings won the NHL title. They were all honored together at a breakfast of champions at the Masonic Temple in Detroit.

The legendary Leroy Satchel Paige, pitching for the Kansas City Monarchs in 1942. *Photo courtesy of the Associated Press.*

was at least as good. He would have been a big winner in the big leagues. But we still beat them, 1–0.

The man who owned the Oxford team won $1,500 betting on us against the Monarchs. We played the Monarchs on a Sunday, and I was paid my normal $75 plus an extra $100 the owner gave me because I won that bet for him.

Playing for that team almost cost me my final year of eligibility in basketball and baseball at Kansas State. Mike Ahern was the athletic director at Kansas State at the time, and he was also on the board of the Amateur Athletic Union. He heard that I pitched against the Kansas City Monarchs for a team from Oxford, Nebraska. He knew I wasn't from around there, so it sounded fishy to him. Ahern launched an investigation. Since he was a big football fan (and didn't give a damn about basketball or baseball), he waited until after the football season was over to start the investigation.

Ahern was a pompous, egotistical guy who took great care to preserve the image that had earned him the nickname "Honest Mike." He didn't want anybody to be able to look at his record and point to any wrongdoing, so he tried to get me kicked out of school. But he couldn't get anything on me because there was no record of me playing for Oxford (although there *was* a record of an Eddie Leroy). Honest Mike was able to get one of my Kansas State teammates, Billy Meissinger, kicked out of school because he played under his own name. Ahern hauled me into his office on several occasions to try to get me to confess, but I played dumb, and he didn't have anything to back up his suspicions.

My first exposure to playing town-team baseball came when I was only 15. Norcatur High School didn't have a baseball team, so I was limited to playing football and basketball for my school. The town baseball team, made up of all adults, recruited me to play for them, much to my mother's chagrin.

She didn't want me playing on the town team for two reasons. First, some of the players drank and chewed tobacco and she did not think I should be exposed to that at such a young age. Second, the games were scheduled on Sundays, and she believed that a boy's priorities should be elsewhere than the ballfield on Sundays. She relented and let me play on one condition: I had to go to Sunday school in the morning before playing any baseball.

We didn't get paid a nickel to play for the Norcatur town team, but some town folks made money on us, and others, of course, lost it. We would go to nearby towns, and a group of people would always go with us to watch the game. People from our town would bet on us and had no trouble finding takers.

If not for the existence of town-team baseball, I never would have played a game with black athletes. In all my years of playing football, basketball, and baseball, those two games I played against the Kansas City Monarchs were the only games I ever played with or against black athletes.

My last year in professional baseball was with the St. Louis Browns in 1942. Blacks were not allowed to sit in the grandstand in St. Louis. All the faces in the grandstand and all the faces on the field were white.

Of course, that doesn't mean I never played with an athlete victimized by prejudice. Don't forget, I was a teammate of Hank Greenberg's.

Chapter 11

Our Hank

I was proud to call Hank Greenberg a teammate and a friend during my six seasons in Detroit. We didn't think of him as Hank Greenberg, the Jewish superstar. We just thought of him as our superstar, our slugger, our Hank.

Back then Mildred and I and several other players lived in the same apartment complex on Chicago Avenue. There was a sign there that read "Restricted." I didn't know what it meant, and neither did Mildred. We didn't give it much thought. Finally, one day I asked somebody what it meant. We were told it meant, "no Jews allowed." Why, we thought that was the craziest thing we had ever heard.

We were born in Kansas, and there weren't any Jewish people out there. Where we came from, this notion that a person should be treated in a different manner based on his religion was a completely foreign concept. It wasn't until I got into baseball and visited all the big cities that we discovered there was animosity between the Southern boys and the damn Yankees, the Catholics and the Jews and the Protestants. But on the team we were never mixed up in anything like that. We were all teammates, and teammates were family.

Anti-Semitic sentiment ran high in certain parts of the country back then, and Greenberg was a target for a great deal of abuse. He kept his feelings about it all to himself, though, because that was the way he was. He just wanted to blend in.

There was one incident that occurred in Detroit that I remember very distinctly. The White Sox were in town, led by player/manager Jimmy Dykes. They could be a pretty mouthy group at times, and were capable of nastiness.

On this particular day, while Hank was running down to first base in front of the White Sox dugout, somebody hollered something along the lines of calling him, "a big, yellow Jew bastard." I believe that was the terminology used. Hank came back to our dugout and didn't say a word about it.

My locker was the second one down from Hank's, so I was familiar with his postgame routine. He normally went into the trainer's room for a rubdown after games. He was very flat-footed, and his feet were always killing him, so he always had our trainer, Denny Carroll, rub them down.

On that day, he altered his routine. He came in, took his outside shirt off, left his sweatshirt on, put on his slippers, didn't take off his pants, and walked out the front door of the clubhouse. I thought he was probably going outside to meet some friend who left word he wanted to see him, since visitors weren't allowed in the clubhouse. He was gone for a while, and I didn't think anything of it when he came back in the clubhouse, went about his normal routine: got his rubdown, took his shower, and got dressed to go home.

It wasn't until the next day that one of the White Sox players told me where Hank had gone when he walked out of our clubhouse in his shower slippers. He had paid a visit to the White Sox clubhouse, looking to exact revenge on the cowardly, mouthy jerk from the other team.

I was told that Hank walked to the door of their cramped clubhouse and said, "I want that guy who called me a yellow Jew bastard to get on his feet." Nobody confessed, so he walked slowly around the room and stared into the face of every man in there. Nobody blinked. Nobody moved. Nobody breathed.

Hank didn't say another word. On his way out, he stopped at the door and looked back at them, then walked out of there and returned to our clubhouse.

That guy with the big mouth was the luckiest guy in the world in my opinion, because if he had stood up, there's no telling what Hank might have done to him. Strong as he was, Hank could have killed the guy.

If the White Sox players hadn't talked about what happened, we never would have known about it. That's the way Hank was. He never was looking for any sympathy and never wanted what he had to put up with to hurt the team in any way. The comment must have really gotten to him for him to go in there like that, because Hank rarely let it show when something was eating at him on the inside.

I can recall another incident where Hank boiled over, and this time, though he wasn't aware of it, he had an audience. We were down in Bradenton playing an exhibition game. Hank played for the first couple of innings, then took himself out of the game because of a headache. He really felt lousy, so he went out to the bus, lay down, and went to sleep for the rest of the game.

We had a pitcher who had spent most of his career in the minors until he perfected a blooper pitch later, when he was with Pittsburgh. His name was Truett Sewell. He had red, wavy hair and a smart-ass disposition. He wasn't the sort of guy you would throw your arms around or anything like that, but all in all he was a decent enough guy.

After the game was over, we got on the bus and the guys were laughing and joking and playing around. Hank had his head over to one side and was sleeping. Sewell was behind Hank, and he hit him on the head, saying, "Come on, Greenberg, wake up. You slept all afternoon."

"Truett, don't do that," Hank said. "I've got a hell of a headache. Please don't do that again."

But sure enough, pretty soon Sewell reached over and hit Hank again. "Come on Greenberg, wake up," Sewell repeated.

Hank never said a word.

We went on to Lakeland and pulled into the Lakeland Terrace Hotel. Hank got off the bus, never changing his even expression, and stood at the door. When Sewell got off the bus, Hank grabbed him by the front of his shirt and took him around the side of the hotel, where he thought nobody could see them. However, we *could* see them while we were getting off the bus.

Hank slapped Sewell across the face and pretty near busted his skin open. "When I tell you to leave me alone, you leave me alone," Greenberg said. "I don't ever want to have any problems with you again, and don't you ever forget it."

Hank just wanted to get that straightened out. He never said a word about it to anybody, and he never bad-mouthed Sewell, either. Sewell was traded to Pittsburgh shortly after that, and he wasn't missed. He was finished in the Tigers' organization after that incident.

Hank was an extremely tough guy, but he never showed that off. He wasn't one to lose his temper. He was probably the most highly respected player on the team. He was just a real first-class guy, a handsome, down-to-earth gentleman.

Greenberg's religion became an issue during the pennant race of 1934 because two major Jewish holidays, Rosh Hashanah and Yom Kippur, fell in September that year. The big story in all the newspapers was whether Hank would be able to play during the two holidays.

Nobody wanted him to play on Rosh Hashanah more than I did, because I was pitching for us that day in Boston. The suspense as to whether he was going to play lasted right up to the brink of game time. He didn't take batting practice, and he wasn't in uniform. But shortly before game time, he put on his uniform and was in the lineup.

I beat Dusty Rhodes that day, 2–1, in 10 innings. Let me rephrase that: it was Hank Greenberg who really beat Dusty Rhodes that day. Greenberg homered twice, both off of Rhodes. Typical Hank. He always rose to the occasion.

He did not play on Yom Kippur, the Day of Atonement, because the leading rabbi in Detroit advised him that Yom Kippur should be spent in prayer. He was, however, allowed to play on Rosh Hashanah, the Jewish New Year, because it was a festive day.

We were all pulling hard for Hank in 1938 when he was chasing Babe Ruth's record of 60 home runs in a season. It would have been great for baseball if he could have gotten the record, and it would have been great for the Jewish community as well. It would have upset a lot of people if Hank had broken Babe's record, because he was Jewish; it would have delighted a lot of people too, and for the same reason.

As far as the rest of the Tigers were concerned, his being Jewish had nothing to do with how we felt about the record. We all wanted him to break it because he was our Hank—a teammate and a friend. He was on pace to get it until he ran out of gas late in the season and finished with 58 home runs.

We also wanted Hank to beat that record because we knew how hard it had been for him to become a great player. It didn't come as naturally to him as it did to most of the other stars. He had those big, flat feet and was a little clumsy, a bit awkward. He had to work and work—nobody worked harder at becoming a better baseball player than Hank Greenberg.

Hank came up from the minors in 1933 and replaced a fellow by the name of Harry Davis at first base. (Davis wasn't much of a hitter, but he was a great little fielder.) Hank was the Most Valuable Player in the Texas League in 1932, but I assure you that it wasn't because of anything he did in the field. He couldn't catch a pop fly when he first came up with the Tigers. Every time he would try to catch a pop fly, he would throw his head back. Those pop flies gave him fits. Del Baker was the manager of Beaumont when Hank led that team to the Texas League title, and he later came to the Tigers as a coach. Hank went to the ballpark at 9:00 every morning and had Baker hit him pop flies with a fungo bat. I bet Baker hit Hank Greenberg a million pop flies. Hank was determined to perfect the art of catching a pop fly, and he worked so hard that he got to the point where he could catch those things in his jockstrap.

Hank also made himself into probably the best first baseman in the league. He was a big target, so tall with such long arms. I still have one of the big, long mitts he had made for himself. He wanted me to have it for some reason when he was done with it.

Part of the beauty of baseball is that on any given day even a banjo hitter might just swing the bat with more power than one of the greatest sluggers in the history of the game. August 14, 1937, was just such a day. The St. Louis Browns were in town for a doubleheader and we clobbered them by scores of 16–1 and 20–7. Jerry Lipscomb, a second baseman, was brought in to pitch in both games to spare their bullpen. I hit two home runs off him in one game. Hank batted against him four times and couldn't hit the ball out of the infield. After it was over, I went up to Hank in the clubhouse and said, "Here, you want these two home runs of mine? I don't need them."

Despite that game, Greenberg managed to drive in a league-leading 183 runs in 1937, the same year Charlie Gehringer led the league with a .371 batting average.

Hank came from a great family. His father was in the textile business in New York and was very successful. Hank became the idol of all the young Jewish boys in Detroit and he lived up to that responsibility with the way he conducted himself.

But he was no gentleman when he had a bat in his hands. He had a real knack for driving in runs and was an especially dangerous hitter with men on base. He swung the biggest bat in an infield that had to be the most productive of any in history. At the very least, the right side of the infield had to be the best of any ever to play the game. I'd like to hear someone name a better duo than Hank Greenberg and Charlie Gehringer on the right side of the infield.

Chapter 12

Take Good Care, Charlie

Charlie Gehringer, as popular a man as ever wore the Detroit Tigers uniform, died January 21, 1993. His wife, Jo, about 20 years younger than Charlie, never has been able to let go of him, and it's easy to see why. They were meant for one another, as compatible as a hot summer day and a sweaty glass of ice-cold lemonade.

A devout Catholic, Jo still attends 7:00 mass every morning of the year. She always finishes her day the same way: she picks up the picture of Charlie at her bedside, kisses it, tucks herself in bed, and dreams all night about the quiet man to whom she brought so much happiness.

Charlie is buried at the mausoleum where anybody who is anybody among Catholics in Detroit is buried. Massive place. Crypts on both sides of the hallway. It's the sort of place where a visitor is never alone, forever kept company by the echo of every footstep.

When I visited, it was just Jo and me and the clicks of our heels resounding in the marble hallways. Nobody else happened to be visiting at the time. Crypts to the left. Crypts to the right. We came to one offset that said, "Charles C. Gehringer." Jo placed her hand on it.

"Charlie," Jo said in a gentle tone. "Elden's here. He stopped by to see you." If Jo's heart had lips, they would have been moving, because that's where every word she spoke originated.

"Elden and Mildred are staying at the house for a few days, Charlie," Jo said. "I'm so glad to have them. I wish you were here with us. We miss you so."

Jo urged me to say hello to Charlie and have a chat with him. I obliged. "Jo's well, Charlie. I don't want you worrying about her. She misses you terribly. We all do. But she's going to be fine. We'll see to that."

It wasn't much different from any conversation with Charlie, who was as quiet as he was clean-cut. Never drank or smoked or anything like that. He always did all the listening, anyway.

"I'm still playing a lot of golf, Charlie," I said. "I still can hit the ball a long way. I just can't do it with as much consistency. The nice thing about getting old though, Charlie, is it's easier to beat your age."

I talked on and on about our days together with the Tigers, just as if Charlie were sitting right there with us. It put Jo at ease, hearing an old friend talk about old times.

When we got ready to go, Jo got up and put her hand on Charlie's crypt. Then I got up, did the same, and said, "Take good care, Charlie. Be good."

It was kind of an eerie experience.

During his playing days, Charlie had it all—speed, power, a great glove, good looks, unequaled popularity—everything, that is, except a mate. In Jo he found the perfect one.

Charlie didn't get married until late in life because he didn't think it was right to settle down and go off on his own when he had his mother to care for. He lived with his mother and his half-sister, a retired nun. It was no place to bring a bride. It wasn't until Charlie reached his early fifties that he married.

Charlie told me that living with those two women wasn't always an easy thing to do—especially going home to them after a tough game. He'd take the collar, go 0 for 4, and when he got home his half-sister would say, "What's the matter, Charlie, aren't you trying?" That would drive him crazy. Then his mother would always say, "Charlie, why don't you get a real job someplace, instead of this baseball nonsense." Here he was, the man every boy with a baseball glove and a dream wanted to be, and his mother didn't think her son even had a real job. But it turned out to be a blessing that Charlie felt the obligation to his mother, because otherwise he wouldn't have wound up with Jo.

Charlie's mother died when he was in his late forties, and he didn't meet Jo until after that. She was a secretary at Chrysler Corporation, and didn't know anything about Charlie Gehringer the baseball player. That didn't impress her a bit. Charlie had to chase her, and that never happened when he was playing ball. He was a handsome guy and the most popular player in town. Girls were falling all over themselves to get at Charlie. But not Jo. Charlie was a salesman to her, nothing more. He just fell in love with her, and she was a great, great wife to him.

Jo tells the story of how they were driving along in the country one day early in their marriage. Jo looked at him, overcome with happiness, and said, "Charlie Gehringer, I just love you to death."

Charlie, as was his custom, didn't say anything. That didn't seem so unusual to Jo, quiet as he was. Then, along about 20 minutes later, Charlie broke the silence.

"You do?" he said. "Why?"

That was Charlie. Never one to waste words. Always one to make them count.

Charlie's dry sense of humor went a long way toward keeping us all in a good mood in the dugout. He had a way of breaking the tension at the times when we really needed that.

One of those times came when we were facing Herb Pennock, once a great left-handed pitcher for the Yankees. It was the 1933 season, and Pennock's better days had passed him by. He was at the end of his career by then, and he couldn't have hurt you if he had hit you right between the eyes with a fastball. All he was throwing that day were these little spinners, little curveballs, and once in a while he'd try to sneak a fastball by you.

Ray Hayworth, one of our catchers, whose grandson is now a prominent Republican congressman from Arizona, couldn't hit Pennock with a handful of sand over the years. For some unknown reason, Pennock just had his number. Hayworth was a mild-mannered guy, but it just drove him crazy the way Pennock owned him. Hayworth would work himself into a sweat when Pennock was pitching. He looked worried sick just thinking about the prospect of facing him. The harder he tried, the worse he did. It was a big joke among the players, the way Hayworth became another man at the sight of Pennock.

Hayworth's first time up, Pennock jammed him, and Hayworth hit a little dribbler to third and was thrown out. Next time up, Pennock got him out on a harmless little pop fly. Third time up, Hayworth was consumed with rage and intent on exacting revenge on the man who caused him so much angst. Villages have been leveled with the sort of wind Hayworth generated on the cut he took against Pennock. Unfortunately, he hit the ball about three inches from his thumb, and it was just another harmless little pop-up. Pennock stood perfectly still on the mound, didn't move an inch, and caught the ball.

Ray went down the line, kicked the first-base bag, and mumbled to himself all the way into the dugout. None of us said a word because Hayworth was so upset. We knew this was serious business, and we kept our distance.

Hayworth was buckling up his shin guards, putting his chest protector on, toweling himself off, and cursing himself the whole time. "If I can't hit a no-good old pitcher like Pennock then I ought to just give up baseball for good," Hayworth mumbled.

Gehringer was sitting right next to him, arms folded, as relaxed as can be. He looked at Hayworth with an expression that defined sympathy. "I know exactly how you feel, Ray," Gehringer said. "When they rob you of a hit with a great catch like that, it's really tough."

The whole dugout broke up laughing. For someone so quiet to say something like that at such a tense moment was the funniest thing you ever heard. Finally, even Ray started laughing. Charlie had broken the tension with just one sentence.

H. G. Salsinger was one of the more talented sportswriters to work in Detroit. He always wore a hat, smoked a cigar, drank beer, and ate onion sandwiches. Excellent writer, highly respected, and a nice, quiet man. He wrote one of the funniest columns I've ever read in a newspaper. It was a fictional conversation between Charlie and Chief Hogsett, one of the American League's better relief pitchers.

In the story, they had just finished eating dinner and were discussing their plans for the rest of the evening. At about 7:30, Charlie said to Chief, "Would you like to see a show?"

At 8:00, Chief said, "Well, I wouldn't mind seeing a show."

At 8:30, Charlie said, "Well, what would you like to see?"

At 9:00, Chief said, "It doesn't matter to me. Whatever you'd like to see is fine with me."

At 9:30, Charlie said, "It's getting kind of late."

At 10:00, Chief said, "Yes, it is. Maybe we'll just stay here and visit."

I'd say Salsinger did a pretty fair job of capturing those two guys.

No sir, Charlie Gehringer wasn't one to go around talking about how great he was. He didn't have to promote himself. He was so damn good only a fool wouldn't notice he was among the very best in the game.

One of the irritating things you see today is the sportscasters and sportswriters talking about how middle infielders never used to hit with power. It's as if guys like Charlie Gehringer never existed, in their minds. Gehringer had power. He had whatever the situation demanded of him at the plate. A left-handed hitter, Gehringer scored a league-leading 134 runs and drove in 127 in 1934, the year we won our first of two consecutive pennants.

If there was a better all-around player in the American League, then I don't know who it could have been. Gehringer

Charlie Gehringer, right, pictured here with Ray Forsyth. *Photo from the personal collection of Elden Auker.*

had a .320 lifetime batting average, led the league with a .371 average in 1937, and always had good extra-base power.

And numbers just don't do justice to how Gehringer demoralized his opponents by doing something to beat them, at the plate or in the field, just when they thought they had him beat.

A pitcher wasn't at an advantage when he got two strikes on Charlie. There wasn't a better two-strike hitter than him. He was like Wade Boggs and Tony Gwynn in that respect. Those two-strike hits are the ones that really eat at a pitcher, and he had so many of them.

He was the same way in the field. He had an uncanny knack for positioning the hitters, and the hands of a magician. No such thing as a bad-hop grounder in the vicinity of Gehringer. His hands would adjust so quickly, so smoothly, the bad hop was barely visible to the audience. It was just another out. His robotic efficiency in the field led to the nickname "the Mechanical Man."

Gehringer teamed with Billy Rogell to form one of the greatest double-play combinations of all-time. They excelled defensively and offensively. They had different personality types, but when a grounder was hit up the middle, they were in perfect synch with each other.

Rogell is one of the funniest men I've ever known. He was always happy when the schedule brought us to New York because that meant he and Flea Clifton could spend their nights at the movie theaters watching westerns. They went to two or three westerns a night.

Billy loved to hunt, and I used to go to his cabin in the northern part of Michigan to go deer hunting with him. Once when I arrived there, Billy was wearing a 10-gallon hat, cowboy boots, and a holster with a pistol on each side. I never laughed so hard in my life.

Rogell was one terrific infielder, but Gehringer was in a class by himself. The way he consistently turned sure base hits into outs broke the spirit of the other team time and time again.

Nobody was more disheartened by the magical glove work of the Mechanical Man than Lyn Lary, the Yankees' shortstop. We were in New York playing the Yankees one day when Lary had the misfortune of hitting the ball on the ground, always a mistake when Gehringer was in the neighborhood. His first time up, Lary hit one out of Hank Greenberg's reach. It was a groundball racing for right field, a sure single. Gehringer had other ideas. He ranged way over to the first-base side, scooped it up, and fired to first in time for the out. Lary hit one just by the pitcher's mound his next time up. Charlie ranged way to his right, almost in back of second base, and threw Lary out at first.

Lary stopped dead in his tracks, put his hands on his hips, looked at Charlie with disgust, and hollered at him, "Gehringer, you bastard. You're just like horseshit. You're all over the place."

I'll never forget that day. I'll have to remember to remind Charlie of that the next time I join Jo at the mausoleum for a visit with my dear old friend.

Chapter 13

Temper, Temper

Many of my fellow players lived in Florida in the winter, and we often got together to play golf in various leagues and tournaments. Babe Ruth, Dizzy Dean, Heinie Manush, Lloyd Brown, Mickey Cochrane, and a number of others played. Even if we were enemies on the baseball diamond, we were friends on the golf course.

Nobody was more entertaining to watch on a golf course than Wes Ferrell, the big right-hander for the Cleveland Indians, Boston Red Sox, and Washington Senators. Ferrell was a nice fellow who was unfortunately burdened with one of the world's worst tempers.

Ferrell and Paul Waner, an outfielder and left-handed hitter with Pittsburgh, challenged Gerald Walker and me to a $50 Nassau match. We accepted the challenge, although those were very high stakes at that time. Walker came from Ole Miss and was a real competitor. He had about a 5 handicap, while mine was about a 3.

When Waner golfed, he carried a pint of whiskey in his bag and would sip from it all the way around the course. One story that made the rounds about him was that, after leading the league in hitting one year, the owner called him in and told him he didn't appreciate that he had been drinking throughout the season. The owner said he wanted Waner to sign a contract that forbade him from drinking, for which he would get a bonus. He signed the contract. When the new season started, Waner couldn't *buy* a hit for the first two or three weeks, so the owner called him back in and told him to forget about that clause. He started drinking again, and the hits soon followed.

Walker and I went down to Sarasota to play Ferrell and Waner in a match at Bobby Jones Country Club; we beat them for $200. We beat them on the front side, we beat them on the back side, and we beat them on the press.

Ferrell had to borrow my driver to tee off on hole No. 9 because he had broken all four of his woods in his fits of rage. "Have a new set of woods for me and meet me on No. 10," he told his caddy. When we got to the 10th hole, the caddy was waiting with the new set of woods. We had a fore caddy with us that day as well, and he was standing out near the brook that ran across No. 10. It would have been very hard, almost impossible, to reach that brook, because you had to hit the doggone thing almost 300 yards to get there. Even for Ferrell, who could really hit the ball, that was a tremendous poke.

Ferrell stepped up to the tee with his brand-new wood and hit it right on the screws. We stood there and watched it, and told him, "That ball's in the water."

"In the water?" he replied. Pretty soon, the fore caddy took his finger and pointed it down, to signal that the ball had indeed gone in the water. Ferrell picked up that brand-new club. He had hit only one ball with it, and had hit that ball perfectly. But he slammed that wood against the cast-iron arrow they had at all the tees. The head of the brand-new club popped right off.

Everybody in the American League was familiar with another legendary Wes Ferrell temper tantrum. It happened while he was pitching for the Indians against the Philadelphia Athletics at

Elden Auker and Gerald "Gee" Walker, left, defeated Wes Ferrell and Paul Waner in a golf match, prompting one of Ferrell's infamous tantrums. *Photo from the personal collection of Elden Auker.*

Cleveland Stadium. Jimmie Foxx came to bat late in a scoreless game and hit one in the upper deck in left field to beat Ferrell, 1–0.

Ferrell came onto the bench burning up after that inning was over. Nobody dared say a thing to him for fear of triggering that temper. He sat there in the dugout, wiped his face off with a towel, took his fist, balled it up, said, "Ferrell you dumb . . . " and hit himself in the jaw, pretty near broke his own jaw. He knocked himself right off the bench and fell flat on his face. His teammates had to go over and pick him up.

Ferrell was traded from Cleveland to Boston to Washington, and his temper made every trip with him. He was pitching for Washington one day when I was with the Tigers; his brother, Rick Ferrell, was catching him. The usual mid-afternoon Washington rain shower hit and they had to cover the field. Washington had scored five runs in the third inning. When they were putting the tarp on the field, I thought Ferrell was going to go crazy; he had a five-run lead and a good chance to win the ballgame. "Would you guys hurry up and put that thing on!" he was yelling to the grounds crew.

The rain soon stopped and the sun came out bright as can be. We resumed play. Ferrell went back out there with runners on second and third, one run in, Hank Greenberg at the plate, and Rudy York on deck. He needed one more out to get out of the inning. They decided to put Greenberg on to load the bases and then pitch to York. York smoked a grand slam into the fourth row of seats out in left field to tie the score, 5–5.

Ferrell watched that ball go into the stands. He stood on the mound and tore the little finger off that glove of his. He took the next finger and tore that off, and he took the next one and tore that off, too. When he got to the extra web for the thumb, he tried to tear that off and couldn't do it. So he's out on the mound, standing on his glove, trying to tear it in two. He finally gave up and threw his glove into the stands.

His brother Rick had just the opposite temperament. I got to know Rick well when he was my catcher in St. Louis. He later became vice president of the Tigers. Rick was the most easygoing guy in the world, but on that day he was angry too, mad as hell at his brother for making a fool of himself out there.

"Come on, give me the ball," Wes hollered to Rick.

"Play ball!" the umpire called.

Since Wes didn't have a glove on, Rick rolled the ball out to him. Wes stomped over, put his foot on it with his spikes, ground it right into the ground, and kicked it.

"Give me a ball," he hollered again to his brother.

Now Rick was really fed up with his hotheaded brother. He got a ball from the umpire and fired it out to Wes, who caught it with his bare hand. The sound that made, it's a wonder he didn't break every bone in his hand. Rick must have thrown it 60 mph.

Wes still wouldn't take a glove. He stood out there and pitched without a glove and got the out he needed. The inning was over and he came in, picked up a bat, went over to the water cooler, and smashed that thing to bits. My God, water flew all over the place. After he busted the water cooler, he went inside to the clubhouse and when he got in there, the clubhouse boy was scared to death. He came in there raving mad. He got his clothes off and went in and took a shower.

He came out of the shower and went back to his locker, and he's yanking at his clothes, talking to himself. When he flipped his pants out of his locker, his gold pocket watch flew out of his pocket and hit the floor. The clubhouse floor had a mat so that you wouldn't slip on the hardwood floor. The watch hit the mat first and then rolled onto the hardwood floor. The clubhouse boy ran over to pick it up.

"Leave that watch alone," Wes told him. He pulled on his pants, stomped over, and put his heel on his pocket watch. He ground that watch right into the hardwood floor.

Many of the most memorable games I worked were against the Indians, and Ferrell wasn't the only pitcher for Cleveland who was known for his temper. Johnny Allen had a terrific temper too, and it was in full bloom on the final day of the 1937 season. Allen started that game with a 15–0 record. Whistlin' Jake Wade, a young left-hander who came into the day with a 6–10 record, was working the game for us. They couldn't hit the ball out of the infield against Wade that day, and he beat Allen, 1–0. Wade was just great that day. Allen was so mad, I thought he was going to slit his throat. From what we heard, Allen tore the clubhouse apart that day.

When I was with the St. Louis Browns, Bobby Feller and I pitched the first night game there, at Sportsman's Park. He struck me out four times. I struck him out three times, but he did hit a home run off of me. There wasn't an easier place in the league to hit a home run than to right field at Sportsman's Park. Feller was late on his swing and hit a little pop fly that fell just over the right-field fence.

Now, every time I see Feller, that home run gets a little longer. "Remember that home run I hit off you in the first night game in St. Louis?" he asked, last time I saw him.

"Yes, I do," I said.

"Remember I hit it over the pavilion in right field at Sportsman's Park?" he asked.

I wasn't going to let him get away with that little slice of revisionist history. "You hit it over the pavilion?" I echoed. "It was a little pop fly to right field."

It wasn't his bat that got Feller into the Hall of Fame. I never saw a man throw a baseball as hard as he did.

The Indians always had tough pitchers to throw at you, from Wes Ferrell to Johnny Allen to Bobby Feller. The one constant for them through those years, the one man who pitched with all three of them as an Indian, was Mel Harder.

Bob Feller, who threw a ball harder than any man Elden Auker ever saw. *Photo courtesy of the Associated Press.*

He was some pitcher. Feller threw harder than Harder, naturally, but Harder threw harder than most. He had good control,
a good fastball, and an excellent curveball. Just my luck, I always
seemed to get matched up against Harder. A big right-hander
from Beemer, Nebraska, Harder won 223 games. His total would
have been 224 if I hadn't gotten out of a jam one memorable
August night in Cleveland in 1940.

I was pitching for the St. Louis Browns and the stands were
packed. Night baseball still had that fresh, new-car smell about it.
The atmosphere that night was very alive, very festive. It was
probably about the fourth duel of the season between Harder
and me.

I had him beat 2–1 going into the ninth. They loaded the
bases with nobody out against me. Fred Haney, manager of the
Browns, let me stay in the game to try to finish what I had started.

I got the final three hitters out, two on strikeouts and one on
a pop-up. Looking back, I guess I helped out my old friends
with the Tigers. The Indians finished second to the Tigers that
year by one game.

Don Barnes, a man the players truly respected and liked, was
the president and owner of the Browns. He always came on the
road with us. Mr. Barnes came into the clubhouse after the game,
and he had wet his pants. He was so excited he actually peed his
pants! He reached into his pocket, pulled out five $100 bills, and
gave them to me.

"That was the greatest game I ever saw in my life," he told
me. It didn't matter to me that those bills might have been a little
damp. I was happy to take them.

Chapter 14

My Favorite Roommates

I'll never forget the knock on our front door in Birmingham, Michigan, early one evening. Knock . . . knock . . . knock. I turned the porch light on, but still barely recognized the disheveled man standing in front of me: rumpled clothes, dirty white shirt, badly in need of a shave, hair pointing in every direction, smelled like a damn brewery. Looked like hell. Looked like a tramp. I stared at Tommy Bridges and the face of shame stared back.

Tommy and I roomed together on the road for six years with the Tigers. I didn't see Tommy have a drop to drink in those six years. The bottle found him after we went our separate ways, and it never let go.

"Tommy, for God's sake, come on in," I said. "Mildred, honey, Tommy Bridges is here." Mildred threw her arms around him, treated him as if he hadn't changed a bit, as if he had just walked off the mound after winning a World Series game. She gave him a hero's welcome.

It couldn't have been easy for Tommy to come see me in the condition he was in. He was a proud man and he cared about what I thought of him.

Tommy never even went downstairs for a drink when we roomed together. He was a wonderful man, a really nice fellow, and he had the best curveball I ever saw. It was like it rolled off the edge of a table. That was the pitch that made him a 20-game winner three seasons in a row (1934–1936) when he was our ace. Schoolboy Rowe and I backed him up.

Tommy came from good stock. His father was a doctor in Gordonville, Tennessee, and his grandfather was a doctor, too.

Tommy was a good family man in our years together with the Tigers. He called home from the road every night. He was always asking his wife, Caroline, how their daughter Evelyn was doing. He so worried about that daughter of his. All Caroline would have to tell him was that Evelyn had a little temperature and Tommy would be up all night, tossing and turning, pacing, worried sick about his little girl. He was really fanatical over that child.

Tommy went to the University of Tennessee, but he never did graduate. Every time I see one of those T-shirts you see nowadays, the ones that say, "Baseball Is Life," I think of Tommy Bridges. Baseball was everything to him. I guess once he could smell the end of his playing career on the horizon, the scent of liquor was the only thing that could kill that frightening odor.

Charlie Gehringer told me that after I was traded to the Red Sox, Tommy never drew another sober breath. He roomed with Al Benton, a relief pitcher from Oklahoma who came to the Tigers from the Philadelphia A's with a reputation as a hard drinker. Tommy took right up with him. Gehringer told me that they didn't even come downstairs for dinner. They drank their meals.

So it came as no surprise to me that on the day Tommy came to my door in need of a friend, he looked about 60 when he was only 45 or so. "I guess you heard I've been drinking, Elden?" he said.

"Yes, Tommy, I've heard all the stories," I replied. I didn't have to tell him what stories I meant. I'm certain he knew, and there was no point in rubbing salt into his wounded pride. One tale that made the rounds was that after Tommy lost his stuff and was dropped from the big leagues, he was pitching in the minor leagues for Seattle, and was pitching drunk. He went out to the mound one night, started to wind up, and fell over. He was so drunk he couldn't even stand up.

It was there, in the minor leagues, that Tommy got himself into trouble. A newspaper reported that a man caught Tommy in bed with his wife, took out his gun, and shot at him. Tommy not only lived to tell about it, he went on to marry the woman. That's whom he was married to when he paid us the visit in Birmingham.

Tommy told me that he was cleaning up his act and had a job interview lined up in Toledo. "I need $125 to buy some new clothes and get straightened away," Tommy said. "I'm never going to have another drink."

"That's not going to get you very far, Tommy," I told him. "I'll give you $500, or $1,000. I'll give you whatever you need. Is $125 really enough to get you straightened away?"

"No, that's all I need," he said. I don't know where he came up with that figure, $125, but that was the figure he kept stating.

"OK, Tommy, I'll tell you what," I said. "I want you to sign a note for the $125. If in six months you write me or call me collect and you tell me you haven't had a drink, I'll cancel the note and you can forget about paying me back. If you take a drink with any of this money and I find out about it, you owe me $125 for the rest of your life. I've got this note and I expect you to pay it, because I'm not giving you this money to buy liquor."

"Don't you worry about that one bit. I've had my last drink," he assured me.

A day later, a story in the paper reported that the police found Tommy Bridges passed out on his front lawn. He had cashed the check at a bar on Telegraph Road, about 10 miles from my house. He went out drinking directly after that. I still have that canceled check somewhere among the mementos from my playing career.

I guess it was about another dozen years or so until I saw Tommy again, at an Old-Timers game against the Yankees. Again, he looked like hell, looked a lot older than the rest of us. I didn't say anything about the money and neither did Tommy. It was a sad, sad deal, what happened to Tommy Bridges. He was such a fine gentleman in the years we roomed together.

I think it's important for players, even with all the money they make today, to build an identity outside the game. Otherwise, you're not prepared for life after your skills have vanished. A man needs a challenge to keep his mind churning and his pride burning. Baseball was Tommy's life, and without it, he just didn't seem to know who he was.

On some nights the Tigers sent Tommy ahead to the next town to get extra rest for his next start. On one of those nights I had the pleasure of rooming with George "Birdie" Tebbetts. He was one of the more memorable roommates I ever had, even though we only roomed together one night. He was nicknamed Birdie because he had such a high-pitched voice and was always chirping, never stopped talking. And his voice carried for miles.

We were in New York to play the Yankees and I was scheduled to start the game the next day against Red Ruffing or Lefty Gomez. I always pitched against Ruffing or Gomez.

Mickey Cochrane sent Bridges home to Detroit to get extra rest because he was starting the first game of our next homestand. Art Sheehan, our traveling secretary, asked me if I wouldn't mind letting a young catcher from Providence College room with me. The Tigers were helping Tebbetts get through school; he was going to join the organization as soon as he finished his education.

When I came back from the ballpark, a little redheaded kid was alone in the room, and I took him down to dinner. He told me all about his family and how he was doing at Providence. We went back to the room and I got into my pajamas, jumped in bed, and read the *New York Post*. Long after I had finished reading the newspaper, he was still fidgeting around, restless as can be, pacing the floor. Finally I said something.

"Hey George, shouldn't you go to bed?" I asked.

"Mr. Auker," he said. "I'm so embarrassed."

"About what?" I asked.

"Well, you know, I always say my prayers before I go to bed," he said. "I don't really know what to do." He had said his prayers every night of his life before going to bed.

"You go over there, get down on your knees on your side of the bed, and I'll get down on my knees next to my bed," I said. "I'll say my prayers and you say your prayers." I got down on my knees next to my bed, bowed my head, and said my prayers. He got down on his knees next to his bed and said his prayers.

He got up and said, "Thank you very much, Mr. Auker." And he went right to sleep. Can you imagine that? He was such a devout Catholic that he just couldn't bring himself to go to sleep before saying his prayers.

The next morning we went downstairs to have breakfast at the hotel and then went to Yankee Stadium with Schoolboy Rowe and a few of the other guys. The subway let you off near center field, so we had to walk all the way around to the entrance.

In New York, nobody ever needed to remind you where you were; the kids who flocked around you for autographs there had a distinct edge, a streetwise manner that suggested they had lived beyond their years. They had a certain rough charm about them. Half of you wished they were more polite and the other half of you was grateful they weren't because of the entertainment value of it.

On this particular morning there were a number of kids who wanted autographs from us. George was walking all by himself, carrying a little bag with his clothes from home, staying close to the stadium wall.

"Why don't you get his autograph," I said, pointing to Tebbetts. "He's a ballplayer. He's a Detroit Tiger. His name is George Tebbetts. He's a catcher." A bunch of the kids ran over and got his autograph, and he got quite a thrill out of that.

I didn't have the heart to tell Birdie what one of those New York kids said: "He's not a Detroit Tiger. I know all the Tigers and he's not one of them."

"Well," I told that boy, "he's going to be a great catcher in the big leagues some day."

"I'll wait," said the boy, New York to the bone. "Now give me your autograph."

Tebbetts broke into the big leagues with the Tigers late in the 1936 season and retired from the Indians in 1952. He later became a manager, scouted for decades, and was one of the most well-liked men in baseball for years. When Birdie joined the Tigers and we'd go to Boston, his mother would bring a cake into the clubhouse for us as a way of thanking us for taking care of her boy.

I happened to talk to Birdie about two weeks before he died. He thanked me for catching his first game. He told me he was eternally grateful to me for making him feel comfortable enough to say his prayers and for telling those kids that he played for the Tigers. That was the first autograph he ever signed.

If you don't miss Birdie Tebbetts, then I guess that's just because you never had the pleasure of meeting him.

I had the best of luck throughout my playing career when it came to roommates, and my luck was never better than when I played for the Boston Red Sox in 1939. Mildred and I named our only child James Emory Auker, which should tell you all you

George "Birdie" Tebbetts, right, with Hank Greenberg. *Photo courtesy of the Baseball Hall of Fame, Cooperstown, New York.*

need to know about what I thought of my Red Sox roommate, James Emory Foxx.

Jimmie Foxx was one of the nicest men I ever knew. Big-hearted, would give you the shirt off his back. He was also one of the greatest power hitters ever to play the game. The year we roomed together, he batted .360 and led the league with 35 home runs and a .694 slugging percentage. He scored 130 runs and drove in 105.

Those would be remarkable statistics for a man under any circumstances. If only people knew what personal hell his wife put him through that year, they would have been even more impressed.

It was 2:00 A.M. in our shared room when the phone rang. Again. I knew who it was because it was always Mrs. Jimmie Foxx when the phone barked in the middle of the night. That's what she wanted to be called: Mrs. Jimmie Foxx, the famous baseball player's wife.

She never did come to Boston that year. I never did meet her. I only saw a picture of her and she was beautiful, a really stunning woman. And a real pain in the neck, too. A social climber was what she was, and Jimmie didn't care for that at all. It was very important for her to be associated with the upper crust. She was always haranguing him in the middle of the night, getting him so upset that he didn't know what to do.

She fell in love with a mainline banker from Philadelphia. She was trying to get a divorce from Jimmie, and was accusing him of all sorts of things he never did. I roomed with him and I knew where he was and where he wasn't. If he had been up to no good, I would have known about it. But that didn't stop her from taking him for every penny he had.

Adding to his stress, Jimmie had purchased a golf course with a business partner and the damn thing was a real drain on his wallet. They always wanted more money, more money, more money from him. That deal was always eating at him.

That was a tough year for Jim, except at the plate. All his troubles ceased when the only thing standing in his way was a pitcher.

Of all the great hitters I faced and teamed with—Ruth and Gehrig, Greenberg and Gehringer, Williams and DiMaggio—nobody showed me more than Jimmie Foxx did one day in St. Louis.

Dogged by hay fever, he was having a lot of sinus trouble. He had asthma and often would have trouble sleeping because he would get so plugged up. I woke up in the middle of the night and he was in the bathroom, tending to a relentless nosebleed. It was bleeding like hell. I got up and asked how long he had been in there. He guessed it was about a half an hour.

"We've got to do something about this, Jimmie," I said.

"Ah, it'll stop," he said, tough as ever. But it didn't stop, so I called the trainer and told him to come up to our room. He stuffed Jimmie's nose with cotton and it finally stopped, but not until he lost what must have been about a quart of blood. It scared the daylights out of me.

We always went downstairs and had breakfast together around 7:30, but on this morning he was so sound asleep after his rough night that I quietly slipped out of the room and ate alone. When I returned to the room he was just waking up.

I told him he should stay in bed. "We're only playing the Browns," I told him. "We ought to be able to beat them without you."

"Ah, I'll see how I feel," he said. "You go on to the park. I'll see how I feel."

We had taken batting practice and were ready to get the game started when in walks Foxxy. He came in and put his uniform on, but hadn't taken any batting practice. His first time at bat, he hit a line drive into the center-field bleachers at Sportsman's Park. It was a 450-foot shot if it was a foot. He hit a line drive out there like you never saw. How the hell he did that, I'll never know. He was one strong boy, could really hit a ball hard.

We used to wrestle once in a while, and Jimmie could break you in two. He hit 534 home runs in his career and it was no secret where his power came from. Foxx could take his arm and make a muscle that would curl up damn near to the size of a cannon ball. Jimmie Foxx was a beast with a bat in his hands, a big, strong guy on the outside and soft as silk on the inside.

I remember one day when I wish Foxx had stayed in his hotel room. He was playing for the Philadelphia A's and I was pitching for the Tigers. I had a perfect game going until he led off the eighth with a double off the wall. We were leading 13–0 at the time, so the only suspense left was whether I could get into the history books. When Foxx banged that ball off the wall, the crowd booed him pretty good, and a lot of people got up and headed home. I'm sure he broke up a lot of no-hitters in his day, plenty of them with home runs.

We would go out after a game once in a while and have a beer or two, but I never saw him drink much at all. I never met a nicer guy in my life. I never heard Jimmie Foxx say a bad word about anybody. He was always smiling, had a great sense of humor.

He was another one who never set himself up for a post-baseball career, and it came back to haunt him. We lost touch after we were out of the game and I'm told he took to the bottle, same as Tommy Bridges. I didn't hear much about him, but I was told he was trying to coach a team in the All-American Girls Professional Baseball League and was broke and drinking heavily. I was told he died choking on a piece of meat, destitute.

He deserved such a better ending than that, for I never knew a finer man than James Emory Foxx, my roommate, a man who gave me so many pleasant memories and a name for my only child.

Chapter 15

The Splendid Rookie

I've heard so many theories about why Ted Williams ran afoul of the Boston baseball fans early in his career that I could write a book about it. It would be a fiction book, though. I never hear anyone talk about the night the real seed of ill will was sewn by a mean-spirited man armed with a poison pen.

Bill Cunningham was a sportswriter who graduated from Dartmouth College. That was the big deal with him. I guess we were supposed to be impressed. He was known as the dean of sportswriters in Boston. Cunningham drank a lot. He always wore a gray fedora hat and he always had a cigar in his mouth. That was his trademark. Whenever the cartoonist sketched him in the paper, he always had on his fedora and was chomping on a cigar.

Cunningham was determined to put a pox on the house of Ted Williams.

I don't know if the real story about the origin of Cunningham's vendetta against the great Ted Williams has ever been told. I happened to be there when it all started. I was in my first year with the Red Sox in 1939, Ted's rookie year.

Lefty Grove and his wife, Jimmie Foxx, Fritz Ostermueller and his wife, Bobby and Monica Doerr, Ted, Mildred, and myself had gone to dinner that evening. Afterward, we were talking about going to play some putt-putt golf and were choosing up sides, trying to make the teams fair. Ted was sitting in a big, over-stuffed chair with his leg hanging over one armrest and his arm hanging over the back of the chair.

We were all talking away, warmed by our overstuffed bellies, without a care in the world. Well, Bill Cunningham came down the elevator and walked up right in the middle of us. He didn't excuse himself. There was no, "Pardon the interruption." Nothing like that. He just walked up to Ted and said, "Well come on, Ted, let's go upstairs and get it over with. All the baseball fans in Boston are waiting with bated breath to hear the story about the kid from Minneapolis. Might just as well do it now as any time."

Ted never moved. He just sat there still as could be. Stared right at him without blinking. Then he uttered the words that would lead to his being mistreated by Boston fans for years.

"Mr. Cunningham," Ted said, "I'd rather do it later because I never give interviews to sportswriters when they've been drinking."

I can still hear the paralyzing silence that fell over that hotel lobby.

Ted was right. Cunningham had been drinking. He had finished his story for the day and it was obvious to all of us that he was half-blind. That wasn't the point, though, to Cunningham. He took it as a real put-down. None of us knew what he was going to do, but we all knew right away how deeply he had been insulted. He just turned around and walked away.

That guy Cunningham, I don't think he ever had an interview with Ted Williams, although he spent the entire summer writing stories about him. He was the guy who really got the Boston fans down on Ted. He knew exactly what he was doing and he never let up. Any time Ted struck out, he would make that the focal point of his story. Never wrote a good word about him. He had the perfect name, for he was both cunning and a ham.

The more bad things Cunningham wrote about Ted, the harder Ted hit the ball. The harder Ted hit the ball, the more bad things Cunningham would write about him. Cunningham was a caustic guy, caustic as hell. Just couldn't say anything good about anybody. And poor Ted was his favorite target. Ted would hit a home run with the bases loaded and strike out twice and Cunningham would write about his strikeouts. Never, ever praised him. That got under Ted's skin, whether he wanted to admit it or not. I don't think Ted said a word to Cunningham that whole year.

Cunningham wrote for the *Boston Globe* and Harold Kaese wrote for the *Boston Herald*. Kaese was a very, very nice guy. Harold was on the case for the *Herald*, and Cunningham was on Ted's case.

"What the hell's the matter with Cunningham?" I asked Kaese once. "Why doesn't he get off Ted's ass, for God's sake? This is ridiculous. He's making a fool of himself."

"Yeah, I know it," Kaese said. "He's really got it in for Williams." I knew where it had started, but I didn't say anything to Kaese about that.

Years later, when Ted gave the finger to the Boston fans, and spit on them, and did some things he never should have done, it could all be traced back to that one night. Cunningham went out of his way to poison the Boston fans against Ted. After a while, he grew tired of the unfair treatment and he fought back.

Ted didn't do a damn thing wrong that night. He was just a young, 20-year-old kid who liked to drink Coca-Cola, laugh, and joke around, a loosey-goosey guy taking those long, graceful strides in the outfield before the game.

Ted was a great guy to have on the team. All that mattered to him was winning that day's ballgame. But thanks to Cunningham, not everyone saw it that way.

That was the only year I spent in Boston, but it was also one of my most memorable years in baseball, even though I had difficulty playing for our controlling player/manager, Joe Cronin. It was that clash with Cronin that caused me to request a trade after a year of teaming with Williams, Lefty Grove, and Jimmie Foxx.

Here's how I got there in the first place: Boston had a third baseman coming up by the name of Jim Tabor. He was coming off a great year in the American Association and had nothing left to prove at the Triple A level. He was ready for his shot in the big leagues. That meant they had no place for Pinky Higgins to play. Detroit needed a third baseman because Marvin Owen was in poor health at the time and was retiring. So the Tigers traded me to the Red Sox for Higgins in order to fill their third-base void. That's how I ended up in Boston for the 1939 season.

I was the new kid on the block and wasn't up on the organization, but the Red Sox players knew all about the hotshot young outfielder who was in spring training with us. He had played out on the West Coast, then played for the Red Sox farm team in Minneapolis. I guess he set every record there was to set in the American Association. Home runs, batting average, runs batted in. He just tore up the league. All the sportswriters and all the players who had been with the Red Sox the previous year were up to date on him, but it was the first I had ever heard of Ted Williams.

The sportswriters were all watching him closely. They called him the Kid and the Splendid Splinter and all that. He had a lot of nicknames. He was a tall, skinny guy who had a tendency to stand in such a way as to make himself look shorter, one foot out in front of the other, one shoulder cocked higher than the other.

I've never seen a young ballplayer who had his mind on baseball as much as Ted did. We had long dressing mirrors in the clubhouse and every time there wasn't someone in front of that mirror, you'd see Ted standing over there with a bat in his hands, hitting some dry line drives or home runs. He was always swinging that bat. That was part of the landscape of the clubhouse. Lockers, showers, Ted Williams taking dry swings. If you didn't watch yourself in the dugout you were liable to get hit in the head by one of Ted's swings.

One thing about Ted that was different from any other rookie I ever saw was that he was inquisitive about the other players in the league, especially the pitchers on other teams. He was always asking things like, "What kind of a pitcher is Red Ruffing? How does Lefty Gomez work? Ted Lyons, what kind of pitcher is Ted Lyons? What's his best pitch?" He'd go through them all, top to bottom, as if he had a checklist in his mind. He'd just interrogate you about every pitch. When we got ready to go north at the end of spring training, I think he knew as much about the opposing pitchers as some guys who had been in the league for 10 years. I really believe that. He was just such a great student of the game.

Ted didn't only know every pitcher in the league; he made damn sure he knew every hitter in the league, too. I never saw a coach move him around in the outfield. He moved himself around. He knew the hitters as well as anybody, even when he was only a rookie. He knew where they were going to hit the ball. When I pitched he knew that Luke Appling would hit me a certain way, Lou Gehrig would hit me a certain way, Red Rolfe would hit me a certain way. He would come in or back up, move to left-center or toward the line. They didn't have to move Ted. He studied those hitters better than they did. Today, with the computers they have, they'll show a graph that shows the hitter has hit 45 balls to right field, 32 to center, 18 to left. Ted didn't need any computer and he didn't need any graphs. He had it all stored between his ears.

Cunningham had to have known how prepared Ted was for games, but he never shared that with his readers.

Anyone who says Ted Williams didn't have the physical tools for greatness is dealing in fiction, but it is true that his greatest baseball tool was his mind. One hit he got off me that I'll never forget illustrates that. It was my first year playing for the St. Louis Browns, in 1940. It was August, I think. It was hot as hell, that much I know for sure. I had Lefty Grove beat 2–1 at Fenway Park. Johnny Pesky, a rookie then, was the first guy to bat in the ninth.

Elden Auker in his St. Louis Browns uniform. Auker pitched the first night game at Sportsman's Park. *Photo from the personal collection of Elden Auker.*

Harlond Clift was our third baseman. Pesky came up, dumped one down the third-base line, and caught Clift flat-footed. Ted was the next guy up. Bobby Swift, my catcher, came out to see me on the mound.

"What do you think you'll be throwing him?" Swift asked.

"I don't know," I said. "Let's keep the ball low and outside where he can't hit it and we'll see what he's trying to do with it."

I threw a ball 18 inches off the ground, 6 or 7 inches outside. Well, Williams stepped out there and hit the ball into the center-field bleachers, just like you'd hit a 2-iron. It was still going full blast when it hit the bleachers. I never had a ball hit like that off of me in my life. Ted was laughing as he went around the bases and the game was over. I started walking to the tunnel. Ted was in front of me, standing and laughing.

"Get away from me, you son of a bitch, before I punch you in the nose," I told him. And I meant it. I was hot. He was still laughing.

"I know what you told Swift," Ted said. "You said: 'Let's keep one low and outside and see what he's going to do with it.' You threw that pitch exactly where I was looking. I knew what you would do as soon as I saw Swift go out there."

That shows you how Ted was always thinking. As a rookie, he'd sit there on the bench, watching, and he'd say, "He started the last four hitters off with a fastball." Or, he'd say, "He started the last three hitters off with a curveball." Other guys would be fooling around, not paying any attention to what was going on. Ted would be totally into every pitch.

He was so intense as a youngster. I never saw a more intense ballplayer. He never smoked. He never drank. He was such a clean-cut kid. He'd drink a soda, but never a beer. He kept himself in tip-top physical condition. Ted was like a coiled spring, always ready to go. Always full of life, so loud and energetic. And so consumed with the game of baseball.

Elden Auker partakes in pitchers' fielding practice with the St. Louis Browns at spring training. *Photo from the personal collection of Elden Auker.*

Ted told me his mother worked at the Salvation Army, scrubbing the floors. When he talked about his family, his mother was usually the topic of conversation. He was so intent on taking care of his mother. It was one of the first things he ever told me. "The first money I earn, I'm going to give it to my mother to get her out of the Salvation Army," he said. "If there's anything left, I'll take it. But the first money I earn, she gets it."

I think he made $6,000 or $6,500 that first year, and I'll bet you he sent $5,000 of that home to his mother. He wouldn't spend a nickel on himself. Whatever necessities he had to buy to get along with in everyday life, that's about all he bought. Soap, shampoo, toothpaste, food, and shelter. That was about it. No fancy cars or anything like that for Ted Williams. That wasn't Ted. He didn't even have a car.

He didn't have a necktie to his name and he had but one sport coat, an old brown one, which he rarely wore. Whenever he did wear it, he would wear an open-neck shirt. He was the first one in the major leagues to wear an open-neck shirt. It became his trademark, but he wasn't trying to make any fashion statement. He wasn't making a statement of any sort. There was all sorts of speculation about why he didn't wear a dress shirt and tie, why he started the open-collar look. Some people tried to say he thought he was special and thought he didn't have to follow anybody's dress codes. Like he was bigger than the game. That sort of rubbish. Nobody on the team ever said anything about it. We knew the reason Ted wore those shirts. He didn't want to spend the money to buy dress shirts and neckties. He wanted his mother to have the money. We all admired him for that.

Ted stayed at a hotel in Boston and so did Jimmie Foxx, who was my roommate on the road. Mildred and I looked out for the two of them because they didn't really have anybody taking care of them at all that year. Oh, I guess it was about four times during that summer of '39 that we had Ted and Jimmie out to the house for some of Mildred's fried chicken. Ted was just like a little kid up at the house, whooping it up, always laughing and joking. He had a great sense of humor. I guess about the only time he didn't talk baseball at the ballpark was when he was telling other guys on the team that they hadn't eaten fried chicken until they'd sampled Mildred's.

As a kid, Ted was a little naive, a little vulnerable. You couldn't help but want to protect him. Everybody looked after him like he was their very own kid. I don't think he ever had a date the whole year. He wasn't crawling around at night at all. Baseball dominated his thoughts, night and day. I don't think he thought about women much, on the road or anyplace. He was always around the hotel and he'd go to bed early. He didn't talk about anything else except baseball. You couldn't be with him two minutes without him wanting to know about a certain hitter or a certain pitcher. He was in his element with baseball, outside his element with anything else. Something about him made you want to watch out for him.

You could see right off the bat that this kid was something special. He had such potential. I'll never forget my first trip back to Detroit with the Red Sox after spending six seasons with the Tigers. Sure, it was nice seeing my old teammates and returning to Briggs Stadium, where I had been in two World Series. But that's not what made the trip so memorable. Ted made it a day I'll never forget.

They had just built a second tier in right field at Briggs Stadium to enlarge the seating capacity. I had roomed with Tommy Bridges for six years with the Tigers. I went to see him before our first game of that series.

"Who's this kid Ted Williams you've got over there that the sportswriters have been writing so much about?" Bridges asked me. "Is he everything that they're talking about?"

"He's good," I said. "I'll tell you what, Tommy. I'll bet you before we leave this ballpark, he'll hit one over the right-field roof."

"I'll have to see that to believe it," Tommy said.

He saw it, and he had no choice but to believe it.

Ted hit one out of the ballpark, over that right-field roof, in his first time at bat. First time it was ever done. I looked across the way at Bridges, who was in the other dugout, pointed at him, and gave him an I-told-you-so smile.

I saw Ted hit a lot of balls a lot farther than that one. He hit balls farther than anyone I ever saw. Quick wrists, that's where he got his power. He worked that thing like it was a toothpick. He never swung until the very last instant. He had such a hell of an eye. He umpired the game, really. It used to be a joke in the dugout. The pitcher wouldn't get a borderline pitch with Ted at the plate and he'd complain to the ump, "Oh, come on, that was a strike." The umpire would say, "Well, he didn't swing at it did he? You'll know when it's a strike. He'll hit it."

As time passes, baseball historians seem to want to label Ted as little more than a bat, a great bat at that, but not a versatile baseball player. Hogwash. He could run. Ted was fast. He took these long strides, like DiMaggio did. They were deceptively fast. DiMaggio could run like a damn deer. Ted wasn't as fast as DiMaggio, but he was fast. You saw some of these outfielders, they could run all day in a half-gallon bucket, they had such short strides. Ted turned a lot of base hits into fly-ball outs with those long strides that covered so much ground in such a short time.

Ted was a terrific teammate. Happy as hell all the time, at least with teammates. He'd get mad at opponents sometimes. And when he did, look out.

We were playing at Sportsman's Park in St. Louis in '39 and Buck Newsome was pitching for the Browns. Newsome was quite a flamboyant guy with a big windup. And he was quite a good pitcher. Ted's first time up, Newsome struck him out. While Ted was walking back to the dugout, Newsome was laughing at him. Ted didn't see it, but when he got close enough to the dugout we all told him Newsome was laughing at him. Once Ted turned around to look at him, Newsome put his glove up to his face to try to hide his laughter.

Ted came in the dugout, wheeled around, and hollered at Newsome on the mound. "You son of a bitch, you won't laugh at me ever again," Williams yelled.

We went around the lineup again and Ted went up there and did what we all knew he would do. He hit a home run and was talking to Newsome all the way around the bases. Newsome wouldn't even look at him. Ted went up the next time after that and hit another home run. He's trotting around the bases again, looks at Newsome, and says, "All right you big bastard, why don't you laugh at that?" Newsome never laughed at Ted Williams again. He made Ted mad and that's never a good idea.

Still, nobody enraged Ted the way Cunningham did. Ted never did say a word to Cunningham the whole year we were teammates, but I did witness him give it to him years later.

Long after I was finished playing ball, we moved from Michigan to Massachusetts. I went out to the ballpark to see Ted in '53 or '54. We were sitting on a travel trunk in the clubhouse when the door opened up and who should walk in but Bill Cunningham. Ted stood up and said to Johnny Orlando, our clubhouse man, "Orlando, get that son of a bitch out of the clubhouse. GET . . . HIM . . . OUT OF HERE." You could feel the anger rising in Ted. "Throw him out the door." Cunningham went into Joe Cronin's office and didn't come back out.

Ted had a stormy relationship with a few of the writers, a good relationship with most of them. All they had to do was talk baseball and Ted would talk with them all day. In the end, Ted won Boston over and, of course, became an icon. And if he was the winner, then I guess that made Cunningham a loser. Yes, loser, that's about right.

Chapter 16

A Splendid Friend

I t's September 21, 2000. The phone rings and I answer it. "Happy birthday, old man," the spirited voice on the other end says. "You son of a gun. You're 90 years old. You're an old man now."

It's so good to hear Ted Williams laugh. I wish he had the chance to do it more often. It's tough to think about him all alone up on that hill in Hernando, Florida, imprisoned, in some ways, by his own fame and his failing health.

"You're about the only friend I have who doesn't want something from me," Ted told me once. "Everyone else wants an autograph from me or wants me to go here for this appearance or there for that appearance. You've never even asked me for my autograph."

"You never ask me for my autograph, so why should I ask you for yours?" I told him.

I meant it. What do I care that he's the last man to have hit .400? That's not why he's my friend. He's my friend because the real Ted Williams is a good, kindhearted man.

Ted was always so strong, so vivacious. It bothers me to think that he can't get around without having somebody help him. His vision used to be so great that he could see the seams of a pitched baseball rotating. That great vision enabled him to spot an enemy plane before it spotted him when he flew for his country in two different wars. Now, the strokes have robbed him of most of his vision; he can't see even six feet in front of himself anymore. He always loved to fish, but he's not able to take fishing trips anymore.

There is nothing wrong with his mind, though. He's sharp and would be happy to talk baseball with you all day long. He's still eager to offer his explanation for why a curveball breaks, and he doesn't care how many aerodynamic studies anybody cites to contradict his argument. He's utterly convinced he's right.

It's a shame that the Ted Williams most of the public knows is the one with the hard shell, the quick temper. The real Ted Williams isn't like that at all. Beneath that hard shell, he's as soft as a baby's skin.

If only people could have seen Ted with his beloved dalmatian, Slugger, they would have known that Ted's gruff exterior is really a disguise. Slugger was always right by Ted's side. That dog meant everything to Ted, and Ted meant everything to Slugger.

"I hope I die before Slugger dies," he said during one of our visits. "I don't know what I'd do without this old dog."

Slugger died. Ted was so broken up about it that he couldn't get out of bed for two days. I waited a while and told him that I was going to bring him a present on my next visit—a dalmatian puppy. "Don't do that," he said. "I don't want another damn dog. All they do is die on you."

I guarantee you not a day passes that Ted doesn't think about Slugger and about how much he misses him.

The Ted Williams Museum and Hitting Hall of Fame in Hernando, established in 1994, has become a big part of his life. The annual induction ceremony and dinner are the highlight of his year. Many of baseball's biggest names make the annual trek to the small, remote town located about 90 minutes north of

Ted Williams, shown here in 1941, remains one of Elden Auker's nearest and dearest friends. *Photo courtesy of the Associated Press.*

Tampa. A golf tournament is part of the annual festivities. I aced a hole in the tournament a couple of years ago. Bob Costas, the master of ceremonies, got a big kick out of that.

"Can you believe that?" Costas said. "Here he is, 88 years old, and he shoots a hole-in-one? And it was his third one. I'm still looking to get my first hole-in-one."

The players who are inducted get such a big thrill out of it and are so pleased to be in the company of Ted. His great performance for the Red Sox inspired so many nicknames. He was the Kid, Teddy Ballgame, the Splendid Splinter. But to me, he is, always has been, and always will be, a splendid friend.

Chapter 17

Streakin' Joe
and the Yankees

The year was 1941, my second of three with the St. Louis Browns. By the time I took the mound at Yankee Stadium on June 26, a nation of baseball fans was captivated by the great Joe DiMaggio's hitting streak. Baseball fans everywhere followed DiMaggio's progress with their ears pressed against their radios.

The streak stood at 37 when I started against the Yankees on June 26, 1941. DiMaggio always had a lot of trouble hitting me. "I can't pick up your damn ball because of that delivery of yours," he told me once, while he dragged on a cigarette in the tunnel. He smoked a lot. I had a screwball and once in a while I would try to get him to chase that. Mostly, though, I would try to keep it in on his hands. A check of the record books shows that I allowed DiMaggio hits in four games during the streak, the 6th, 23rd, 38th, and 51st.

He once signed a picture of himself to me with the following greeting: "To Elden, a tough submarine to sink."

I nearly sunk his streak.

He flied to left in his first at bat against me that day. His next time up, he grounded a ball to Johnny Berardino at second base, and Berardino booted the ball. All the Yankees came to the dugout steps and stared up at the press box. I guess they were trying to put pressure on Dan Daniel, the official scorer. It didn't work. Daniel made the right call—he charged Berardino with an error.

DiMaggio grounded out to third his next time up and, still hitless, was the fourth man due up in the eighth inning. We were trailing, 3–1, and unless we could tie the game or go ahead, DiMaggio wasn't going to have a chance to hit after the eighth.

Red Rolfe reached first on a walk with one out. Tommy Henrich was up next. I don't think I thought anything of it at the time, but since then so much has been made of what he did next. He met with Joe McCarthy, the Yankees' manager, and told him of his plan to put down a sacrifice bunt to stay out of the double play and make sure DiMaggio got another chance to hit. Evidently, it was the first time the Yankees did anything special to accommodate the streak. McCarthy bunted Rolfe over to second base and DiMaggio came to the plate with two outs and a man on second base.

I can honestly say I didn't give a damn about the streak. Why would I? I wasn't making any money off it. *My* streak was all I was concerned about. If I had wanted to end his streak, I could have done that very easily. I would have hit him with the pitch if that were my goal. First base was open. I could have done that, but I wasn't thinking about the streak. I was thinking about getting him out and hoping we could come back and win the ballgame.

DiMaggio hit my first pitch hard. It was a smash down to third base. It glanced off Harlond Clift's shoulder and went into the outfield for a double. The run scored and we lost the game, 4–1. DiMaggio's streak grew to 38 on the way to his record of 56, a record that isn't likely to be broken any time soon.

Joe DiMaggio, who set a record hitting streak of 56, always had trouble hitting Elden Auker's submarine pitches. *Photo courtesy of the Associated Press.*

151

The streak meant nothing to me, and there was no way of telling what it meant to Joe. He never showed any emotion on the field. If he hit a home run, he just put his head down and ran the bases. If he made a great catch in center field, he just threw the ball back into the infield. He was the furthest thing from a showoff.

I enjoyed chatting with him during our playing days, but didn't keep in touch with him afterward. But we did have an enjoyable exchange once during an Old-Timers game between the Tigers and the Yankees at Yankee Stadium in about 1960.

Around the third inning or so, they sent DiMaggio in to pinch hit. Mickey Cochrane, slowed by cancer, managed the game for us. As soon as he saw them send DiMaggio up to the plate, he told me to go out to the mound to pitch.

But once DiMaggio saw me walking to the mound, he turned around and started walking back to the Yankees' dugout. When I saw that, I turned around and started walking back to our dugout. We kept doing that, walking back and forth, putting on a little show. We both were laughing about it.

Finally, he went up to hit. "How are you going to pitch me?" he asked.

"I'm going to pitch you low and behind you," I said. "Be loose." I threw the first pitch behind him, as promised.

"I flew in from Stockholm, Sweden, last night," Joe said. "If I knew I was going to have to hit against you, I would have stayed in Stockholm."

DiMaggio was a great ballplayer and a terrific outfielder. He never threw to the wrong base and had a rifle arm. He was a nice, quiet guy during his playing days and never did anything to call attention to himself.

I was with the Tigers the first year DiMaggio came up, and I remember the play that taught us about his deceptive speed. He had such an effortless running style, which fooled many an infielder.

Billy Rogell, our shortstop, knew just how much he needed to rush in order to make a play and get the runner out. He had a great feel for all the base runners in the league and knew just how to time his throws for the runners. It didn't matter if a runner got down to first base in three seconds or five, Rogell always threw them out by a tenth of a second.

The first time DiMaggio hit a ball to him, Rogell started into that little prance. DiMaggio was gliding down the line with those long strides of his. He was just about at first base before the throw. He almost beat it out.

Back in the dugout, Rogell said, "That guy can really run, can't he?"

He *could* really run. He could really hit and throw, too. He could really *play*.

We always knew we had our hands full playing the Yankees, and there was no one among their many stars who found more ways to beat you than Joe DiMaggio. But they were also tough to beat because they were always so tough up the middle. Catcher Bill Dickey was always a big part of that up-the-middle strength.

I was working a game in Detroit one day in 1937 and Johnny Broaca was working it for the Yankees. Broaca was from Yale; he was quite a guy and also a pretty good pitcher. He was pretty fast and had a fast-breaking curve. It came in straight and then, at the last instant, broke down just a little. He struck me out with that damn little curve my first two times against him. I couldn't hit that pitch with a paddle. My third time up, the first two pitches he threw me were curves and I couldn't touch them. About nine of the ten pitches he had thrown me at that point were curveballs. He had me at 0–2.

I backed out from the plate and said to Dickey, "If a guy can't hit that lousy curve, he shouldn't even be standing up there swinging. That curveball is the worst thing I've ever seen. If you throw it to me again, I'll knock it out of the ballpark."

Broaca threw me a fastball and I knocked it clear out of the ballpark. I mean, that ball was gone. When I came around to home plate, Dickey was waiting for me. "You lying bastard," he said. "You were looking for that fastball and you made me think you were looking for that curve." It was close, but I beat Broaca that day.

The next day I read in the newspaper that Broaca had jumped the ballclub. That loss had brought his record to 1–4, and he wasn't used to losing. He was despondent and jumped the ballclub. He didn't make it back to the big leagues until 1939, with Cleveland.

I saw Dickey shortly after that, and he was laughing. He hollered, "Damn you. You don't only knock guys out of the box, you knock 'em clear out of the league."

Toward the end of my career, the Yankees called up another player, Phil Rizzuto, who would become a pillar of their strength up the middle. He arrived with very little fanfare and eventually made it to the Hall of Fame.

Rizzuto and Jerry Priddy were renowned as a great double-play combination in the minors. Priddy was the one who was considered the better prospect when they came up, but they brought Rizzuto up too, to keep the double-play combination together. Rizzuto turned out to be better than anyone had expected. Priddy bounced around with a few different teams and was always a very good defensive player.

Many years later, I was among a small group speaking at a symposium at Hofstra University that was held to celebrate Babe Ruth's 100th birthday. Rizzuto was to receive an honorary degree in humanities at the symposium.

As he was walking up the aisle in his hat and gown, he spotted me and said, "I want to speak to you after this. I've been waiting for years to see you." He came up to me later and asked if I remembered the first time he had faced me at the plate. I told him

I didn't. He told me I had hit him in the head and he spent the night in the hospital.

"I'm sorry," I told him. "I'm sure I didn't do it intentionally."

"That's OK," Rizzuto told me. "I wasn't that upset. I should have gotten out of the way. But man oh man, if my mother had gotten a hold of you that night, she would have killed you."

Chapter 18

Battling Management

After Mr. Navin died, Mr. Briggs inherited his portion of the Tigers, as per their agreement, and we were left to negotiate contracts with old man Briggs, who might as well have had the nickname Crime. Why? Because crime doesn't pay.

Mr. Navin gave me a $2,000 raise in the middle of the 1935 season to bring my salary to $12,000. During the winter before the 1936 season, Briggs sent me three contracts, but I didn't sign any of them. I sent each one of them back unsigned. I had gone 18–7 and helped the team win the World Series in 1935. I thought I deserved a raise.

We lived in Lakeland during the winter, and Briggs lived in Miami Beach in a great, big home on Collins Avenue. Jo Shevlin, his secretary, called and said the old man wanted me to come down to talk contract with him. I made an appointment to see him, and Mildred and I drove from Lakeland.

I had no way of knowing what was taking place in Detroit before I drove to Miami Beach. The workers at Briggs Body MFG., which made all the bodies for Chrysler automobiles, staged a wildcat strike. The situation became so bitter that the workers at the Mack Avenue plant were setting upholstery on fire and tossing it out the fifth-story window.

"Gee, you picked a hell of a time to come see him," said Briggs's son, Spike, a nice guy who used to travel with the team. "He's been up all night with the strike, trying to deal with the unions. He's not in a very good mood."

Briggs was a multimillionaire who fought to keep every last nickel. He was forever at odds with the unions and didn't think twice about firing workers. He was always firing guys, left and right, wouldn't even blink an eye.

My appointment with him was for 10:30 A.M. Understandably, he was delayed, and I waited until he could see me.

He was sitting in his wheelchair behind a great, big desk. Right off the bat, he asked, "How come you haven't signed the contract I sent you?"

"It's not enough money," I said.

"Well, what do you think you're worth?"

"If you're asking me how much I'm worth that's one question," I said. "If you're asking me how much I want to sign a contract, that's another question." I was trying to make a joke to ease the tension. He didn't laugh and didn't appreciate the small talk. He was too busy to bother with small talk.

"I want to know how much you want to sign a contract," he said.

"I want $15,000," I said.

Briggs hadn't walked for 10 years, but I thought he was going to get up out of that wheelchair and tear me apart. He had a horrible temper and he swore like a trooper.

"You want $15,000?" he said, incredulous. "How am I going to pay the rest of the ballclub? What makes you think you're worth $15,000?"

I stood up and started to leave. I was determined not to sign a contract for a penny less than $15,000, because that was what I honestly believed I was worth. He went crazy when he saw that I intended to walk out on him.

"Where are you going?" he said through his fury.

"I didn't mean to make you mad," I said. "You asked me a question and I just answered it."

"Sit down," he said. "Why do you think you're worth $15,000?"

"Well, I had a pretty good year," I said. "I won 18 ballgames. We won the championship and I think I played a part in winning that."

"I know that," he said. "I know that."

He pressed the button for his secretary and told her to get the contract and make it out for $15,000. I think he had more important things on his mind and just wanted to get rid of me, so he gave me what I asked for and I was on my way. But he didn't seem to care for me after that. I noticed that from then on he was colder to me.

I always got along with Spike, though. Briggs eventually made Spike the president of the club, even though he didn't know anything about baseball. The old man sent two "body guards" on the road with Spike. They were actually nothing more than spies. They were checking on Spike all the time. Briggs didn't trust his own son.

I chuckle when I hear people say that, in the old days, we played strictly for the love of the game. Wrong. Of course we wanted money. But we had to go about trying to get it differently than today's players do.

For one thing, owners have changed a great deal. When I played, most of the owners knew their baseball, so dealing with an intermediary wasn't necessary. When outsiders came in and bought teams, the owners had to hire presidents and general managers to run the teams. They bought teams for tax write-offs and for ego trips. Not many of them are dedicated to the sport, whereas almost all of the owners used to be passionate baseball men.

We didn't have a union negotiating rights for us and we didn't have an agent or anyone else negotiating our contracts. Every time I negotiated a contract I negotiated with the owner of the ballclub. During my time with the Tigers, I dealt with

Frank Navin until he died, and then with Walter Briggs. I negotiated my only Boston Red Sox contract with Mr. Tom Yawkey and my three contracts with the St. Louis Browns were negotiated with Mr. Don Barnes.

For another thing, the owners held all the cards then. The players hold more of the cards now. When free agency first came in, I was happy for the players. Before that time, the owners owned us as if we were chattel, one of their automobiles or horses. They controlled you. You couldn't do anything without going to them first. You couldn't play for another club. You couldn't even talk to another team.

The rule was that when you signed with a team, you belonged to that team for ten years. If you were traded or sold to another team, the ten-year period would start over and you had no way of getting out of it. Sometimes, if a player had been with a team for nine years and was just about eligible to be free, he would be sold to some other team and there was nothing he could do about it. You could either go where you were traded or retire. They could pay you what they wanted to pay you, send you to the minors whenever they wanted to, trade you whenever they wanted to, and you had no recourse.

Arguments about money and contracts weren't the only disagreements that came up between players and management. There were also differences in playing and managing philosophies, so to speak. I guess I was spoiled by Mickey Cochrane's philosophy of letting a pitcher throw his own game. That could explain in part why I had such a difficult time playing for Joe Cronin, the player/manager in my one season (1939) with the Red Sox.

Joe Cronin was a very nice fellow. He was also a knowledgeable baseball man. His management style worked well enough for him to manage the Washington Senators into the World Series in 1933, Cronin's first season as a player/manager.

He was such a skilled player that he was inducted into the Hall of Fame in 1956. He had credentials. After his playing days, he performed quite capably in his role as league president. I had nothing personal against him. I liked the man. He just wasn't the right manager for me.

He was nervous as hell. He was always kicking the dirt out there at shortstop. After the pitch, he would run onto the mound, grab the rosin bag, throw it down, and say something like, "Keep the ball down. Make him hit the curveball. Make him hit the fastball." He was always on the mound and it just drove us pitchers crazy. I saw Jack Wilson crying on the mound a few times because he couldn't take it. I couldn't concentrate on what I was doing.

Cronin did this to all the pitchers except Lefty Grove. When Cronin would start to walk toward the mound, Lefty would start toward the dugout. Lefty wouldn't even talk to him when he came to the mound, so he stayed away from Lefty.

I had been in the league for six years and I knew how to pitch to everybody, but that didn't stop Cronin from coming to the mound. His favorite advice was, "Don't give him anything good to hit, but don't walk him." Gee, thanks.

I had worked several games before I figured out that Cronin was calling all the pitches from shortstop. He gave the signals to the catcher without me even knowing it. I was working a game against Cleveland, one of my many duels with Mel Harder, and Gene Desautels was catching me. I shook him off several times and he kept coming back with the signal for the same pitch.

I called Desautels out to the mound and asked, "What's the matter with you? When I shake you off, you have to let me throw my pitch."

"Cronin's calling the pitches," he told me. "If you want to shake somebody off, you're going to have to shake him off."

In another game, I was working for us and Lefty Gomez was working it for the Yankees. I bet Cronin made 20 trips to the

Joe Cronin was a skilled player/manager, but he couldn't stop telling Elden Auker how to pitch. *Photo courtesy of the Associated Press.*

mound that day. It seemed as if he came over almost every pitch. "Keep the ball outside on this guy," he would say. "Make him hit the fastball."

Cronin came in one more time and I lost my temper. "Here, you pitch the damn ballgame and I'll play shortstop," I told him. "How about that?"

Evidently, he didn't care for that outburst. He not only took me out of the ballgame, he took me out of the rotation. He sent me to the bullpen and didn't use me again for more than three weeks.

With the Tigers, Mickey let me throw my own ballgame, and Bo McMillin always let me call my own plays when I was the quarterback at Kansas State. It was what I was used to and I thought it was the right way to go about things. I didn't adjust well to having somebody call my game for me and I responded with the worst year of my career. I won only nine ballgames.

After that season, Yawkey signed Cronin to a five-year contract. They had such a good relationship that Cronin named his first son after Tom Yawkey.

Mr. Yawkey called me in after the season and told me he wanted to sign me to another contract. "You just signed Joe up for another five years," I replied. "I can't play for him. Either you trade me or I'll quit baseball. I can't play for Joe Cronin. I won nine lousy games and it was the worst season I ever had. I don't have anything against Joe as an individual. I like him. I just can't play for him. No way."

Yawkey tried to calm me down. "We want you to stay here," he said. "We'll talk to Joe." He told me everything would be all right, but there was no changing my mind.

"It won't do any good," I said. "You can't change Joe Cronin. He's a nervous individual and I don't care who says what to him, he's not going to change. Once the game starts, he's going to be on the pitcher's mound."

I didn't sign the contract and, about three weeks later, I got a call from Fred Haney, who was managing the St. Louis Browns. "I talked to Tom Yawkey and he tells me you're not going to sign with him and you'll quit if he doesn't trade you," Haney said.

"That's right," I said.

"Would you pitch for me?" Haney asked.

"Hell, yes," I said. "I'll pitch for anybody who doesn't tell me how to pitch and stays off the damn pitcher's mound when I'm trying to pitch."

He told me the Browns wanted me. They bought me from the Red Sox and paid $30,000, I think, to get me. I won 16 ballgames for St. Louis in 1940. I had three enjoyable seasons for the Browns and could have played more, but decided to retire for reasons that had nothing to do with baseball.

Chapter 19

The Real World

knew my time in baseball wasn't going to last forever. Even for the greatest players, it never does. I wanted to prepare myself for the outside world before I was done playing, so when an opportunity came along during the winter after the 1938 season, I took advantage of it.

"We're going to stay in Detroit and I'm going to get a job," I told Mildred at the end of the season. "I'm tired of just going to Florida and golfing all winter. I've got to find something to do. The day is going to come when I can't get these guys out anymore, and when that happens I want to have something to do."

She told me she thought that was a good idea.

A friend of mine named Jim Jackson told me he was looking for good men to work for him at his small abrasives firm. He told me I should start working at the plant and learn the business from the ground up. I told him I would give it a try.

"I've got a job," I told Mildred.

"You have? What are you going to do?" she asked.

"I'm going to work for Midwest Abrasive Company," I said.

"What's that?" she asked.

"I really don't know," I said.

"Well, what does it pay?" she asked.

"I don't know," I said. "I didn't ask."

"You mean to tell me you got a job, you don't know what it's all about, don't know what you're going to do, and you don't even know what your salary is? What kind of a job is that?" she said.

"It's a start," I replied.

I was right about that. By the time I finished in the abrasives business, it was 1975 and I was president of the second largest company in the industry.

That first winter I worked in all the departments to see how they made the product, to see what the product was all about. The next winter I went into the sales department. Then I started taking classes in Detroit. I took engineering and mathematics classes: algebra 1 and 2, geometry, trigonometry, calculus. Then I started working in the area of honing gun barrels for antiaircraft gun manufacturers.

The Germans were dive-bombing our ships with these low-flying aircraft and we needed to make 20-millimeter and 40-millimeter guns top priorities in order to combat them. I became an antiaircraft gun specialist. During the 1942 season, when the Browns went to Washington, I spent any time I wasn't at the ballpark at the Washington Navy Yard.

I won 14 games in 1942 and retired after the season because I wanted to devote all my time to the war effort, honing gun barrels. Our job was to make a product that honed the barrel of the gun down to a finish of smaller than three microinches, which is smoother than a mirror. Glass is about four microinches.

Clark Griffith, owner of the Washington Senators, was asked by Commissioner Landis to approach President Franklin Delano Roosevelt about keeping baseball alive. When I retired, Griffith called and told me that he had spoken to Roosevelt, and the president told him that he wanted baseball players to stay in the game because he thought it was good for the country's morale. I told him I appreciated the call, but that I just didn't feel right playing baseball while our men were fighting overseas.

Mickey Cochrane was in charge of the athletics program at Great Lakes Naval Station and he called and asked if I wanted to join him there as a lieutenant, junior grade. But if I was going to fight the war, I didn't want to do it from Chicago.

My decision to retire and do what I could for the war effort as an antiaircraft gun specialist wasn't a good short-term financial decision. I made $27,500 pitching for the Browns in 1942, then went to work for $500 a month after I retired. Looking back, it would have been nice to play a few more years, but I have no regrets. It's better to get started on a second career too soon rather than too late.

I spent 10 years in the American League and more than 35 years in the abrasives industry, but all anyone ever asks me about is my time in baseball. Nobody has ever asked me to talk about bonded abrasives.

My athletic background was as much of a curse as it was a blessing in the business world. It opened countless doors at Kansas State, but at times it also led to misconceptions based on the "dumb and spoiled athlete" stereotype.

We never had much money growing up and I guess I was about the poorest athlete at Kansas State. My last year there I was voted the most deserving athlete, which meant I was awarded the job of selling advertisements for the football program.

Fred Seaton, who years later would become a United States senator and then President Dwight D. Eisenhower's secretary of the interior, was a classmate of mine at Kansas State. His family owned the local newspaper and printed the football program. I received a percentage of the revenue generated from the advertisements.

I called on everybody who had anything to do with any kind of business at all in the area. We had an athlete do the selling because people knew the athletes and rooted for them, and would have a very difficult time saying no to them. It was a very sound plan and it worked. I made $1,200, and that year the football program was the biggest one we ever had. At that time, it was the most money I had ever seen in my life. I was still working at the drugstore, making a dollar a day.

The experience was lucrative, but it did not give me an accurate indication of things to come. Having played in the major leagues did not open as many doors for me as being the local college standout had. I had sensed that this would happen, so when I retired from baseball I did not go to the ballpark for five years. Ty Tyson would always make an announcement when an ex-ballplayer was in the park, and I didn't want to be associated with going to a ballgame during the day, when I was supposed to be working. It was important to me to establish my credibility outside of baseball.

One of the most difficult things I had to do was get the men at Chrysler Corporation, Ford, and General Motors to look at me as an abrasives man. It was a technical business. I could get in to see a buyer because I was a baseball player, but then when I wanted to talk business, they would say, "Well, what the hell do you know about abrasives? If I've got a problem with them, you can't help me." That was tough. I had to prove myself and it was no small challenge.

In today's world, spectators pay to watch millionaires play baseball. But during the golden age of baseball, the only place you could find a millionaire at a game was in the stands.

Henry Ford, the nation's first millionaire, attended Tigers games regularly, and was a big supporter of the Tigers' first World Series champions in 1935. Ford, who died in 1947 at the age of 83, attended the games with his son, Edsel, and grandson, Henry Ford II. His right-hand man, Harry Bennett, was also a regular at the games. The Ford family box seats were right next to the Tigers' dugout.

Ford introduced the Model T in 1909, the same year Ty Cobb led the Tigers to the American League pennant.

The Ford family had a particular fondness for Mickey Cochrane, whom they employed for a time after his playing days were over.

Elden Auker—a businessman, but ever a ballplayer. *Photo from the personal collection of Elden Auker.*

A call I made to Chevrolet Gray Iron Foundry in Saginaw, Michigan, best illustrates the difficulties I encountered getting past stereotypes when making the transition from the playing field to the business world. It was the biggest cast-iron foundry in the United States. They made all the cylinder blocks for all General Motors automobiles sold in the United States. A man by the name of Jack Hantz was the director of purchasing there.

We made grinding wheels that foundries used to grind the castings; that Chevrolet plant bought a lot of grinding wheels, but they didn't buy any from us. I went up there cold to try to generate new business.

I gave my name and my business card to the woman in the lobby and said I would like to see Mr. Hantz. After I waited in the lobby for a short while, she told me to go inside and let me know that his office was at the end of the hall.

Jack Hantz was an old-time foundry man, as gruff as an ocean is deep. He was sitting there wearing an old gray hat with a black band around it, crunched down on his head. He was sitting behind an old rolltop desk and had a big table in front of him.

I stood at the door and he never looked up. I cleared my throat a little, thinking that might get his attention. He still didn't react in any way, didn't even look up. I walked over to one of the chairs in his office and very quietly sat down.

Hantz's office was glass, so you could see the entire office at work outside. There were a couple of women sitting outside and as I looked up, their eyes turned away. They were curious about what was going to happen when Mr. Hantz finally acknowledged my presence.

I sat there and waited and waited and he didn't pay the slightest bit of attention to me. He never said hello to me, and eventually he just got up and walked out of the office. After that, I knew what a Siberian winter felt like. Surely, I thought, even that can't be this cold, this long, this hopeless.

Finally, he came back into his office, sat down, and started writing again, never said a word to me. All at once, he whirled around in his chair and said, "Well, what do you want?"

I started to get up to introduce myself. "Mr. Hantz, I'm Elden . . . "

He cut me short. "I know who you are," he said. "The girl announced you from the lobby."

"I represent Midwest Abrasives," I said.

"I know that," he said tersely. "The girl told me all about that. Now what do you want?"

"Well, I'd like to talk to you about selling grinding wheels to you for your foundry." The look he gave me suggested he considered me as overmatched as a high school dropout applying to become the dean of Harvard Law School.

"Where are all your medals?" he asked.

"I beg your pardon?" I asked.

"You heard me," he said. "Where are all your medals?"

"Sir, I don't know what you mean," I replied.

"Regularly, some broken-down football player or basketball player or boxer comes in here and he's got a vest on and a gold chain going across it. And they've got a football or a pair of boxing gloves or a golf ball or a basketball hanging from the gold chain. Where are yours?"

Stand your ground, I thought. Don't blink. Don't let this man intimidate you. Above all, remain composed.

"I'm sorry," I said. "I guess I wasn't very lucky. I haven't got any medals." He sat there and glared at me, and I didn't have a clue what he was going to say next.

"You're selling grinding wheels," he said. "As long as I sit in this chair you will never sell me a grinding wheel."

"Well, why not?" I asked.

"Because I don't buy them," he said. "See that guy sitting down there in the corner? If you think I'm tough, he's the guy who buys grinding wheels and he is tough. Come on, I'll introduce you to him."

And that guy *was* tough. He was a mean old guy. A salesman would come in, put a cigar in front of him as a gift, and he would throw the cigar back at him. But from that day on, I sold them a bunch of grinding wheels.

A few years went by and Jack Hantz retired. By then, we had started what we ended up calling the Bancroft Salesmen's Club. I went up to Saginaw every Wednesday to call on Chevrolet. A bunch of us stayed at the Bancroft Hotel every Wednesday night and had dinner together.

One night, I made a suggestion to the club that was greeted with mixed responses. "You know, Jack Hantz is retiring," I said. "Why don't we have a dinner for him?"

Half the salesmen were scared to death of him. "That old bastard," a couple of them said. "I wouldn't feed him table scraps."

Finally, the group decided I should talk to him and, if he was agreeable, we would have a retirement dinner for him the following Wednesday. I talked to him the next morning and asked if he would come to a dinner in his honor.

"Oh, I suppose so, if they want me to," he said. "But a lot of those guys don't like me."

"Don't worry about that, Jack," I said. "We'd like to have you." By this time, his hair was all white and he looked older than his 65 years. He had spent his whole life in that foundry and was as tough as a boot.

At his dinner, I walked in with him and they all clapped. The Siberian winter thawed, right before our eyes. His eyes flooded and tears streamed down his face. He stood up and addressed the gathering.

"This is the most wonderful night I've had in my whole life and I'll never forget it," he said. Half the men in the room were crying. We all came to find out mean old Mr. Jack Hantz wasn't so coldhearted, after all.

Every week at the Bancroft Salesmen's Club meetings, we would get up and tell stories. One week, a few years after Jack Hantz's retirement party, when it was my turn to tell a story, I suggested we do something besides entertain ourselves for a change.

"We're all sitting here like a bunch of fat cats, filling our bellies with food, having a few drinks," I said. "You know, tonight there are a lot of kids who don't have enough to eat. Christmas is coming up soon. Every night we come in here, let's each of us put $5 in a pot. When Christmas gets here, we'll have a Christmas dinner for the underprivileged kids in town. We'll go to all the churches in town and have the ministers select the kids. We'll select 100 kids." The manager of the hotel offered to supply the food, and the dinner was held there as well, free of charge.

The next Christmas, 100 kids were treated to dinner and a toy. You never saw anything like it in your life. The great, big ballroom of the Bancroft Hotel had toys all over the place. One of the salesmen, a big, hefty guy from U.S. Steel, wore a Santa Claus suit and gave away the presents.

I never saw kids eat like that in all my life. Those little kids dressed in tattered clothes must have drank 60 gallons of milk. It was the greatest Christmas I ever saw and it became an annual event. Coming up with the idea for that annual Christmas party ranks right up there with my proudest achievements in business.

From a purely business standpoint, the idea I came up with that had the greatest potential for profit never went anywhere, at least not for me.

We were living at the Tanton Apartments on Chicago Boulevard in Detroit, and became friends with two residents there who were in the theater business. One of them was a German baron named Frederick Von Bonham. His wife was a school-teacher, and he sold films for Universal Pictures. He called on all the theaters throughout the state of Michigan. Our other friend in the movie business was a fellow by the name of Ollie Brooks. He was the president of the Butterfield Theaters. At that time there were 131 Butterfield Theaters throughout Illinois, Iowa, Michigan, and Ohio. Brooks was in charge of the entire chain. He was a big-bellied, jolly man who was always enjoyable company. Ollie lived with his girlfriend, Jane, a great gal. Everyone assumed they were married. Not too many people knew they weren't. We knew it because they were very good friends of ours.

Anyway, I had popped popcorn ever since I was knee-high to a duck in Norcatur. I still pop popcorn every Sunday night. Nothing beats popcorn and a glass of milk for a Sunday night snack.

"Ollie, I've got a proposition for you," I said. "You've got 131 theaters you guys operate. I'd like to make a deal with you. I'd like to put a popcorn machine in each one of your theaters. I'll put the machines in." There was a place in Detroit that manufac-tured popcorn machines. I had already asked them if we could

173

work out a deal to lease 130-some machines, and they were tickled at the prospect. I told Ollie I would pay the guy to operate the machine at each theater and it wouldn't cost him a nickel.

"I'll give you a minimum of $1 a night," I told Ollie. "You'll have $131 coming to you every night, whether anyone goes to the picture show or not. At the end of the month, we'll figure it out and whatever profit we make, I'll give you 50 percent of the profit and I'll keep the other 50 percent. We'll keep the books together."

He thought about my idea and I could tell from his expression that he was intrigued. "Let me talk about that with the other board members," he said.

After the board meeting, Ollie told me they had discussed my idea. "Elden, the board thought you had a good idea, but we can't do it," Ollie said.

"Why?" I asked. This was when movies were just becoming popular, and I was excited about the idea of selling popcorn. Naturally, I was disappointed that it didn't fly.

"In the first place, the board feels that popcorn will be a distraction," Ollie said. "People will be trying to listen to the picture and will be distracted by the people eating popcorn. Taking popcorn out of a sack or a cardboard box would make noise and disturb the people and we would get complaints."

That was only half the problem, as far as the board was concerned. "And another thing," Ollie continued. "It would be a housekeeping problem. The people eating popcorn would be dropping it all over the place. It's got butter on it and they would be getting the butter on the seats and on the floor. We'd have to clean it up."

Movie theaters make a big portion of their profit on popcorn sales today. Call it a great idea before its time. I didn't make a nickel off of popcorn. That's all right. It's not as if that makes eating it every Sunday night any less pleasurable.

Chapter 20

You're Away, Mr. President

I had gotten to know Gerald Ford through business and we were supposed to play golf together in the Avco Classic Pro-Am Tournament in Sutton, Massachusetts, one year. That plan was foiled when a senator from South Carolina pulled some strings to get into the group, which included Vice President Ford, Lee Trevino, and Speaker of the House Tip O'Neill.

O'Neill and Ford were quite close. Ford got a big kick out of him, and it was easy to see why. I got to know him when I was living in Massachusetts and Washington, D.C. He could sing Irish ballads like nobody you've ever heard.

Ford told me about a time when O'Neill took two or three shots from a sand trap and couldn't get the ball out. All Ford could see was the top of his head. The ball finally came flying out of there, but O'Neill hadn't used his club to get it out. "That's my hand mashie," O'Neill told him.

I would have enjoyed playing a round with them, but it didn't work out that way. They reassigned me to play in Al Geiberger's group, and we won the tournament. Meanwhile, the senator from

South Carolina got drunk during the round, which incensed Trevino. It was a real fiasco.

When Vice President Ford got back to his office, he wrote me a letter saying that he was very sorry we hadn't been able to golf together. He included a pair of vice-presidential cuff links in the letter. The very next day after he wrote the letter, he became president.

I wrote him back, telling him that I greatly appreciated his letter and that I, too, was sorry we didn't get to play together. I wrote to congratulate him on his new job and wrote, "Oh, by the way, thank you for the obsolete cuff links you sent me."

He responded with another letter and included a set of *presidential* cuff links.

After I retired as president of our division in Westboro, Dresser Industries asked if I would go to Washington for a year to evaluate whether the office there should be enlarged or eliminated. This was in 1975. Mildred and I had just bought a house in Florida, but I agreed to do it anyway. I commuted. I flew to Washington on Monday mornings and flew back home to Florida on Friday evenings.

One day I received a phone message asking me to call President Ford. I returned the message and talked to his secretary.

"Mr. Auker, what we're calling about is the president wants to know if you can golf with him next Saturday out at Burning Tree," she said. Burning Tree was the club that all the presidents belonged to.

"I'll be glad to, but I don't have my clubs here," I said.

"We'll take care of the clubs and we'll send a car out to pick you up," she replied.

"You tell him I certainly accept and I'm very grateful to have the opportunity to golf with him," I said. "We've been talking about this for a couple years so I'll be glad to see him."

I had one more order of business. I had to call Mildred to let her know I wouldn't be coming home the following weekend. She still wasn't feeling 100 percent better from surgery she had recently undergone.

"Honey, would it be all right if I don't come home this weekend?" I asked. "The president of the United States has asked me to play golf with him."

Mildred responded, "Oh come on, Elden. If you want to stay up there for the weekend, go ahead and stay, but can't you at least come up with a better excuse than that?"

"No, really," I said. "I'm not joking."

"Well, if that's the truth, you're welcome to stay," she laughed.

Ford was just as common as an old shoe, just a regular guy. We called him Gerry unless someone else was there, in which case we showed him the respect he deserved and called him President Ford.

Elden Auker says hello to Massachusetts' Governor Francis W. Sargent and President Gerald Ford. *Photo from the personal collection of Elden Auker.*

The public formed its opinion of him as a golfer based on film clips of him hitting gallery members and flubbing his first drive at Pebble Beach. But I played with him a couple of times in Florida after I retired, as well as on that day at Burning Tree, and the truth is that he's quite a good golfer. He was strong. He could hit the ball nine miles and he hit it straighter than most people would have guessed.

He told me about the first time he played at the Pro-Am tournament at Pebble Beach. He said the line of people in the gallery was so long that at the end it seemed as if the fairway was about two inches wide, and he was afraid he was going to shank one and hit somebody. To try to keep that from happening, he gripped down on the club. He dribbled a 50-yard grounder down the middle of the fairway.

I met many interesting people that day at Burning Tree, including Senator Barry Goldwater. His locker was right next to mine in the clubhouse, and he had brought his brother out to golf that day. Years later, it was Goldwater who got J. D. Hayworth, the grandson of my old Tiger teammate Ray Hayworth, started in politics.

We teed off that morning around 9:30 and had lunch inside afterward. President Ford called a man over to have lunch with us and wanted to introduce me to him, but coincidentally, no introduction was necessary. The man was Frank Fitzsimmons, who became president of the Teamsters after Jimmy Hoffa was taken out of office. We knew each other quite well when we lived in Detroit.

During my playing days I was fortunate enough to play baseball with legends before they were legends. And during my years in business, I was able to meet a few presidents before they were presidents.

I was vice president of the National Association of Manufacturers (NAM) and president and chairman of the board of the Associate Industries of Massachusetts. They were political arms of industry that lobbied on foreign and interstate commerce, taxation, and environmental control issues. We always had our annual meetings during the first week of December at the Waldorf in New York. The last night of the week we always had a political speaker of some renown at the annual dinner. President Eisenhower spoke one year. President Johnson spoke another year.

This particular year we had the governor of California as our guest speaker. A crowd of 2,500 attended the black-tie affair. Members of the board and their wives got to meet the speaker and his wife at the reception. I was never one to run up and meet someone like that, but Mildred was anxious to meet the governor's wife. About 35 of the 50 board members and their wives had gone through the line when the lights started blinking to signify the reception was wrapping up. Mildred talked me into getting in line.

Our chairman was a very formal man and he presented us in a very formal manner: "Governor and Nancy Reagan, I would like to present Elden and Mildred Auker."

Ronald Reagan stuck out his hand and said, "Elden Auker, my God, boy am I glad to see you. You probably don't remember me, but I'll remember you for as long as I live."

"Governor, you've kind of got this reversed a little, haven't you?" I asked.

"No, no," he said. "I'll tell you why. In the 1935 World Series, you pitched the first game in Chicago against a fellow by the name of Bill Lee. You were taken out for a pinch-hitter and Bill Lee was taken out for a pinch-hitter and the game went extra innings."

"That's right," I said.

"Do you remember talking to a radio announcer before you went down to warm up before the game?" he asked.

179

"No, no special one," I replied.

"Well, you probably don't remember speaking to the same guy after the game, either, do you?" he asked.

"No, I don't."

"I told you you wouldn't remember me," he said. "I'm the guy who interviewed you. The Chicago Cubs selected me as their official announcer for the World Series." Reagan had been an announcer for the Cubs; he used to re-create the games from the Teletype for station WHO in Des Moines, Iowa.

"It was my first big break and a few years later I ended up in Hollywood," he said. "I'll never forget that game."

I'm told that today's reporters never talk to the starting pitcher before the game. That wasn't the case for us. But the interviews were less formal then. There were none of those, "How do you feel?" questions. It was just casual talk. That day in Chicago there had to have been 25 or 30 sportswriters from all over the country on the field.

I had the chance to meet another president when he was still a senator.

During the war, I traveled to several different places to work on the barrels of antiaircraft guns. One day when I was at General Machinery Ordnance Corporation in Charleston, West Virginia, a senator happened to come to "inspect" the plant.

"That's a nice machine," he said repeatedly. I helped to escort him through the plant and he looked at everything as if he knew what he was looking at.

Senator Harry S. Truman was a very nice man, but he wasn't qualified to "inspect" an ordnance plant. He didn't know a drill press from a honing machine.

Chapter 21

A Day on the *Marlin*

My good friend Dick Steele and his wife Louise joined Mildred and me for a long weekend on Cape Cod early in Jack Kennedy's presidency. We went out to the Cape to play some golf, fool around, and get away from it all. Dick was the publisher of the *Worcester Telegram & Gazette* at the time. I was vice president of marketing for Avco Bay State Abrasives. I started with the company in Michigan in 1946, then went to work out of the corporate headquarters in Westboro, Massachusetts. But work wasn't on our minds during what turned out to be a more interesting weekend than we ever would have predicted.

We checked into a motel around 5:00 P.M., had some dinner, and called it a night. We were going to play golf early in the morning. We already had enough excuses for slicing drives into the woods—we didn't need to add fatigue to the list. The phone rang at about 8:00 A.M., shortly before we were going to head out. It was Dick's secretary.

"Mr. Joe Kennedy wants to get in touch with you," she told Dick. "I kind of hesitated to tell him where you were. I told him you were out. He wants to see you. He's down at the compound and wants you to call him. Here's his number if you want to talk to him."

Dick was a very conservative guy and the *Telegram-Gazette* was the only conservative newspaper in New England at that time. The *Boston Globe* and all the other papers were big supporters of the Kennedys. The family was always after Dick to give them a little help. That's how their relationship started, but it went beyond that. They hit it off and it was easy to see why after watching them spend a day together. Mr. Kennedy and Dick had become good friends over the years, and Dick became friends with the family as well.

Dick called him to see what he wanted. "What are you doing down here?" Kennedy asked Dick.

"Louise and I are here for the weekend with Elden and Mildred Auker," Dick said. I had never met Mr. Kennedy personally, but he knew of me as a baseball player and through his son, Ted. I had Ted out to the plant several times when he was campaigning. Whether it was Democrats or Republicans, we always let the candidates come through and meet the workers. Mildred and I came to know Joan quite well. She was such a lovely young lady.

As I said, Jack Kennedy was president at the time and Bobby was attorney general. Ted was just getting started in the family business—politics.

"I'd like to have you and your wives come over and have lunch with me and go out on the *Marlin*," Joe told Dick, inviting us onto the president's boat. "We'll have lunch and I'll fix you my favorite cocktail."

Dick cupped his hand over the phone, turned to me, and asked if I wanted to go over to the compound in Hyannisport instead of playing golf. I told him sure I would. I loved golf as much then as I do now, the only difference being I couldn't shoot my age back then. Still, I couldn't bypass an invitation to spend the day at the Kennedy compound, to go out on the *Marlin*.

Ted Kennedy, center, visiting Elden Auker's plant during his campaign. *Photo from the personal collection of Elden Auker.*

It wasn't until years later, when the father's predictions about his sons unfortunately came to fruition, that I fully appreciated what a remarkable afternoon I had spent at the Kennedy compound and on the *Marlin* that day.

I don't remember the exact date, but it was the day Ted's wife, Joan, returned from the hospital with their first baby, Ted Jr. He was the child who, years later, lost his leg to cancer.

Shortly after we arrived, Joe gave us a tour of the house. He showed us the big dining-room table where they ate all their meals. They had such a big family, that table must have been 40 feet long. Beautiful table. Must have been at least 20 chairs around it.

Then he showed us a lot of family pictures and talked about young Joe, his oldest son, a fighter pilot who had been shot down and killed in the war. He showed us a number of pictures of handsome young Joe in uniform.

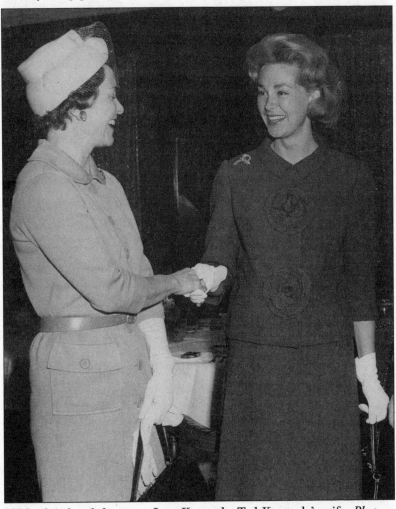

Mildred Auker, left, greets Joan Kennedy, Ted Kennedy's wife. *Photo from the personal collection of Elden Auker.*

An object, about a foot high, on a table piqued my curiosity. It had German words written on it. "What's that?" I asked Joe.

"Well, I'll tell you what it is," Joe said. "When I was the ambassador to the Court of St. James when the war first started, we lived out on the edge of London in a big home out there. This bomb was dropped in my yard by a German airplane."

The English translation of the German note on it read something like, "This is what we could do to you, ambassador, if we wanted to." I couldn't read German, but that's what Joe Kennedy said the words meant.

Joe showed us a number of interesting artifacts he had from his days as ambassador to England and from his years in business. He showed us various things from his friends, a lot of notables from all over the world. We spent probably an hour touring the compound before we went down and got on the boat.

Ann Gargan, his niece, was there with him. His wife, Rose, wasn't there that day. Just Ann, who took care of him. She was showing our wives around while Joe showed us around. Caroline and John John were there playing, but they didn't come on the boat with us. Ann, Mr. Kennedy, and the four of us got on the boat.

A little wire-haired terrier named Charlie Brown was there that day. He was the president's dog, a cute little thing that kept jumping on the boat. "Get that damn dog out of here," Joe said. "We don't want that dog here." They threw the dog off the boat twice and it jumped back on twice. The second time he jumped right onto my lap. "Get this damn dog off of here," Joe groused. "We don't want this dog here."

"Leave him here," I said. "He won't hurt anything. I'll take care of him."

"OK," Joe said. "I didn't think you wanted him on the boat."

He was such a gracious host, so accommodating, a more regular guy than you might have guessed, and not at all afraid to let you in on some of the family secrets. He worried aloud about his sons, maybe because of the fate his first boy had encountered.

On our way out to sea, Joe told us all about how his folks came to the United States from Ireland. He said they had not a penny to their names. They were poor Irish and left for the United States when the potato famine was in full stride. He shared his experiences as a victim of prejudice when he was a boy growing up in Boston.

"We were frowned upon, called trash Irish," Joe told us. "The Italians pretty much controlled the city in those days. All the kids made fun of me in school. They all called me shanty Irish." He really had a complex about that; couldn't stop talking about how they beat him down.

He told us of the trouble he had getting admitted to Harvard and shared with us how he made his first million, as a bootlegger. He used to run the liquor in Boston Harbor during the days of Prohibition. He would go down to Boston Harbor, pick it up, and distribute it to the speakeasies.

When Franklin Delano Roosevelt got into office, Joe wanted FDR to grant him exclusive distributorship in the United States on four liquors: Dewars scotch, Beefeater gin, Balentine scotch, and, I believe, Ronrico rum. Roosevelt got it for him. I think he said they became acquainted at Harvard. Kennedy was a very conservative guy but he was smart enough to go along with a winner, even a winner as liberal as Roosevelt. So he supported Roosevelt, and FDR wound up naming him ambassador to the Court of St. James.

Joe talked about Rose's father—whom he called "Papa Fitz"—the mayor of Boston, who was so popular that he won an election while in prison for bribery or some such backroom dealings. He was really the one responsible for forming the Kennedys' political base with all the Irish people in Boston.

Then Joe started talking about his sons, and an interesting afternoon became downright fascinating. As the years passed, the characterizations of his sons that he had shared that afternoon became more and more eerie.

"Joe, you know, he's really the one who should have been president," Joe Sr. told us. "He was the greatest guy I ever knew. He had more personality than anybody I ever knew. He was a fantastic guy."

He couldn't say enough about Joe; it was obvious that his eldest son was always with him, never far from his thoughts. When he talked about Joe Jr.'s death, the pain that churned inside him was palpable. He relived the futility of that tragedy one more time, welcomed us into his unending horror show. "Useless," he said. "Absolutely useless. He was out and then he went back. He didn't have to go back. But that was Joe. He was going back there and he was going to whip the Germans. He went back and they got him." Whoever it was who killed the son just about killed the father too, broke his heart right in two.

Next, he talked about Jack, but he never did refer to him as Jack. It was always, "the president." His own son and he called him "the president." Can you imagine that?

"The president, well, I don't know whether he'll be a good president or a bad president," he said. "Only history will tell. But I'll tell you one thing: knowing him as I do, he'll be the most stubborn damn president. He'll go down in my book as the most stubborn damn president we ever had."

He told us they used to argue all the time. The president was pretty liberal and the old man was a staunch conservative; they used to go 'round and 'round, never giving any ground, never seeing the wisdom in the other man's ways.

"They won't let us talk politics in the house," Joe said. "At the compound, we have to go outside and talk politics. When people are there and we talk politics, we have to go out in the yard. Boy, we'd almost get into fistfights talking about some issues. He's so damn stubborn, the president."

Bobby, his father said, was the son most like the late, revered Joe. He had such high hopes for Bobby, countered by such deep fears. "Bobby, the attorney general, he's the smartest of the three boys," Joe said. "He and Joe are about the same from an intellect standpoint. Joe was smart. Bobby's smart. He's got a good mind."

What he said next gave me chills then, but that was nothing compared to how the words echoed years later, how they still echo, forever. "You know," he said, "he's been hassling the unions. If he gets out of that job without being killed, he'll be lucky."

Naturally, the moment I heard that Sirhan Sirhan's bullet had ended Bobby Kennedy's life when he was running for president in 1968, I was whisked back in time. I was sitting on board the *Marlin* again, Charlie Brown on my lap, Joe Kennedy speaking. He saw it coming and he knew there wasn't a thing he could do to stop it. He never lived to see it, nor did he have to. He saw it long before it happened.

Joe talked about Bobby going after the unions, but the mob was really what he meant. He never used the word *mob*. He was very careful not to use the word, but you knew that's what he meant.

Finally, he talked about his youngest son and his assessment was every bit as frank and accurate. "Now Ted, he's just starting out in politics," he said. "He has some of the charisma of Joe, but he isn't near as smart as Bobby. He has enough know-how to get along all right. He has a real good personality. He ought to do all right in politics if he just keeps the zipper of his pants zipped shut. That's one of his weaknesses."

We talked some baseball and politics, but it was the haunting forecasts that he shared about his sons that would ring so tragically true through the years.

Nevertheless, it was a very nice day, and he was such an interesting man, so bright, candid, and opinionated. And it isn't difficult to figure out who his son Jack inherited his stubbornness from.

We had lunch and he fixed us his favorite drink—daiquiris, frozen daiquiris. He stirred those up himself. He seemed proud of his ability to make such tasty drinks and he did have a talent for it. We had a nice lunch on the boat.

At about 2:30, Ted came skiing out to the *Marlin*. He got onto the boat with his skis on and rode back with us. There was no need to check to see if he had the zipper of his pants zipped shut—he was wearing swim trunks.

Later I wrote a note to Mr. Joe Kennedy thanking him for a most enjoyable day in the compound and on the *Marlin*. I included a newspaper clipping of a story about me. I still have the letter he sent in reply:

> Dear Elden,
>
> You were very thoughtful to send me along the Sunday *Times*. Mrs. Kennedy loved the pictures and I called her attention to the handsome young fellow in the upper left-hand corner of page 7. I explained to her that the reason the young fellow looked so handsome was because he played baseball in his early days. I must admit that I got no response other than a wide smile. But we old athletes stick together. You did tell me that Ted was making you a visit in January. I'm very appreciative of your invitation to learn something about making a grinding wheel, but to be very honest with you, Elden, that is the very least of my interests at the moment. A new recipe for a daiquiri or a new drink altogether would be of great interest, but a grinding wheel, I'm sorry, is not my line. Charlie Brown is coming back from the vet's today. He has been sick as the result of a fight.

But he's showing up today as Caroline is arriving this afternoon and Ann is running everything in good order. Give my best to your Mrs. And tell her this afternoon I'll hand over the picture of the two good-looking young men to one of the good-looking young men who will be arriving on the president's plane. I'll be up one of these days, probably sometime during the winter or early spring, to visit with you again.

> With my warmest personal regards,
> Sincerely,
> Joseph P. Kennedy

We had planned to get together in Worcester, but he had a stroke shortly after writing that letter and never made it to see us again.

Chapter 22

Swapping Stories

Baseball is a game that can be appreciated long before the first pitch and long after the final out through the telling of stories. Time never travels more swiftly than when listening to a good baseball story.

I was reminded of that fact one night in Brooklyn at one of my favorite restaurants, Bamonte's, the old Brooklyn Dodgers hangout. Mildred and I owe Tommy Lasorda an apology. We kept him up way past his bedtime and must be careful not to do so again. Tommy's so full of energy, I tend to forget he's in his seventies and needs his rest. We were swapping so many baseball stories that before we knew it, it was 2:00 A.M.

One of my favorite stories involves Earl Whitehill, a left-handed pitcher who last pitched for the Tigers the year before I joined the team. Whitehill was noted for having a hair-trigger temper and a pretty wife. His wife's likeness still adorns the side of the Sun-Maid raisin box. You know, the pretty gal in the bonnet. That's Mrs. Earl Whitehill.

As is the case with many ballplayers, Whitehill enjoyed a round of golf. Well, one day he and three other players were golfing in Tucson, where the Tigers held their spring training camp for the last time in 1933. Whitehill was standing there, waiting for the foursome in front of them to finish the hole, when from out of nowhere a ball comes rolling through his legs. Some impatient golfer in the foursome behind them had hit into them. He was livid. "I'm going to go back there right now and punch his lights out!" he told his playing partners.

He was close to doing just that until teammates with cooler heads convinced him to just let it go and count his blessings that nobody was hurt. Whitehill reluctantly followed their advice. Once they got up to the next tee and were waiting to hit their drives, the foursome behind them reached the green, affording them all a closer look at the grave offender of golf etiquette. It was then that Whitehill realized he had made one of the most prudent decisions of his life. His teammates had spared him a painful beating, at the very least. The man who hit into their party was Jack Dempsey. Yes, that Jack Dempsey, the heavyweight champion of the world noted for his lethal knockout punch.

Whitehill earned 101 of his 218 career victories after 1931. Somehow, I think that number might have been smaller if he had acted on his first impulse and set out to exact revenge on the man who had the nerve to hit into him on the golf course. Every time I see a box of Sun-Maid raisins, I think of that story.

One teammate of mine who was always quick with a story was Mickey Cochrane. He brought us more than great wisdom, superior leadership, excellent defensive play, and a lively bat when he joined the Tigers in 1934. He also brought many great baseball memories. Many of them were of the great Lefty Grove. Thanks to Cochrane, by the time I teamed with Grove on the Red Sox in 1939, I felt as if I had already played with him.

One such story involved the great Connie Mack, owner and manager of the powerhouse Philadelphia A's of Cochrane and Grove, Jimmie Foxx and Jimmy Dykes, Al Simmons and Mule Haas, Bing Miller and Max Bishop, George Earnshaw and Rube

Heavyweight champion Jack Dempsey. *Photo courtesy of the Associated Press.*

Babe Ruth was past his prime when the Tigers and Yankees were locked in a pennant race in 1934. Ruth, 39, hit an uncharacteristic .271, with just six home runs and only 36 RBIs.

But even at that point in his career, Ruth still had a flare for the big moment. The Babe's 700th career home run, hit at Navin Field on July 13, 1934, put the Yankees in first place and shoved the Tigers into second.

The Tigers quickly regained the league lead and went on to win the pennant.

The previous year, Ruth had shown his penchant for delivering in the clutch by hitting a two-run home run with Charlie Gehringer on base in front of him to lead the American League to a 4–2 victory over the National League in the first All-Star Game.

A teenage boy named Lennie Beals was at the head of a pack of boys sprinting down Plum Street to retrieve the souvenir. He sold it to Babe for $20 and an autographed baseball. Isn't that about the same amount the guy who sold Mark McGwire's record-setting home-run ball got?

Walberg. Mr. Mack always wore a suit and tie to go with his sailor hat. He always sat in the dugout and never ventured into the clubhouse.

One day Mack's A's were playing the Yankees and the game was a scoreless tie going into the ninth inning. Babe Ruth hit a home run to beat Grove 1–0. Grove went into the clubhouse and tore it apart. He was kicking stools all over the place, banging lockers, tossing aside everything in his path. Nobody on the team said a word. They all just sat there and watched his fit take its course. Finally, he calmed down a little and was sitting in front of his locker with his head down, staring at the floor.

The players had to pinch themselves to make sure they weren't dreaming, so shocked were they at what they next witnessed. Mr. Mack walked into the clubhouse—nobody could believe it. He never came into the clubhouse. *Never.* All eyes were glued on Mr. Mack.

"Mr. Grove," he said. He was a very formal man in

every way and always addressed his players with *mister.* Grove looked up at Mack.

"I would like to talk to you about that pitch you made to Mr. Ruth," Mack said.

Grove exploded. "Oh, horseshit!"

"Yes, Mr. Grove," Mack said. "And horseshit to you!" With that, he turned around and walked out of the clubhouse.

Cochrane also told us stories about what an inspiration Grove was to Rube Walberg, another left-handed pitcher. Walberg used to lose it sometimes late in the game. He would lose a little off his fastball and would get a little wild in the late innings. If Grove noticed that starting to happen, he would leave his seat in the dugout next to Mr. Mack and walk out to the bullpen to start loosening up. Walberg saw Grove out there and knew that if he didn't get it going, he would be out of the game. Cochrane said Walberg's speed would pick up 25 percent when he saw Grove out there.

There were also times when Grove would walk out of the bullpen, walk to the mound, and just take over for Walberg without Mr. Mack even telling him to go in the game.

Lefty was a tough guy on the mound. He could be mean out there. Once he was in Detroit with the Red Sox, and Billy Werber was playing third for them. One of our hitters hit a routine pop fly straight up in the air. Werber got right under it and was standing there waiting for it. Werber dropped it. Grove was so disgusted that he took his glove hand and made a waving gesture at Werber, as if to say, "Go away. Get off the field." I was afraid he was going to kill Werber.

Grove had a great fastball. He could throw that ball right through the wall. He had great control, a good curveball, was stubborn as a mule, and highly, highly competitive. If a hitter really dug in and hit one hard off of him, he would find out what it was like to hit lying down his next time up. Grove would come up and in hard.

Away from the game, Grove was a nice, softhearted guy and a great prankster. He liked to joke around a lot. Tom Yawkey, the owner of the Red Sox, used to come out to the ballpark with some expensive neckties on; Grove would often get a pair of scissors and cut the necktie in two. But during games, he didn't find *anything* particularly funny.

When someone got a hit off of him or he got knocked out of the box one of us would say, "tough luck."

"Tough luck, my ass," he would reply. "It was horseshit pitching is what it was." That was his standard remark.

Grove had an interesting conditioning philosophy. He believed that if you kept your legs in shape and threw every day you would never hurt your arm. He would pitch batting practice the day after pitching in a game and would throw almost as hard in practice as he did in the game. He wore guys out in batting practice. He didn't want them getting hits off of him even then. It didn't matter if he pitched 12 innings in a game, he would be out there the next day throwing and throwing and throwing. He never did get a sore arm. He was still pitching for the Red Sox at the age of 41, and he won 300 games, even though he didn't get out of the minor leagues until he was 25.

Another great baseball storyteller was Bill Summers. He was quite an umpire in his day. He was so respected that he was asked to work seven All-Star Games, and was behind the plate in six of them. And he was every bit as good at telling stories as he was at making calls.

Summers told me of the day he was working a doubleheader at Yankee Stadium and Bobby Feller was pitching the second game. Teams always saved the fastball pitcher for the second game of a doubleheader. This was because the batter would be in the shadows, making it hard to see the ball even with just an average pitcher on the mound.

There was nothing common about Feller. He was fast and he was a little wild. He would throw one behind you, in the dirt, over your head, then down the middle.

Somehow, the Yankees had scored a run off Feller. He probably walked two guys: hit one and threw a wild pitch. They were going into the last of the fifth inning and the ballgame was in the books as an official ballgame. However, it was starting to get dark. This was before the days of night baseball.

Joe McCarthy, the manager of the Yankees, started yelling at Summers. "Call the ballgame," McCarthy hollered. "That guy out there is going to kill somebody the way he's buzzing that thing around."

Summers, as is the case with many umpires, was on the hard-headed side, and was not about to let anyone tell him how to do his job. You yell at Summers to do something and he's going to do just the opposite. You yell at him to call a game and you'll be playing until midnight. Summers was mad at McCarthy for yelling at him.

Well, at this point, Lefty Gomez came to bat. Gomez always carried his bat like you would carry a baby, in his left arm, across his body. He walked up to the plate and the capacity crowd was roaring.

Gomez was probably batting about .050. He couldn't hit the ball back to the pitcher if he was lucky enough to hit it at all. Gomez stepped in the box. Just as Feller got ready to deliver, Gomez struck a match and held it up in his left hand.

"You goofy so and so, what are you trying to do, show me up?" Summers said to Gomez. "You can see him out there on the pitcher's mound."

"Yes, Mr. Summers, I can see him all right," Gomez said. "I just want to make damn sure he can see me."

Another name that often comes up when we get around to swapping stories is Oscar Melillo. The stories almost always center on his fear of animals.

He was with the Red Sox in the 1937 season. Schoolboy Rowe and I were running in the outfield when we noticed a sparrow. Schoolboy threw a ball at the sparrow and killed it. In those days, the players would leave their gloves out on the field after taking infield practice. The umpires would come out and scream "Play ball!" and everyone would run out and grab their gloves. Schoolboy put the dead sparrow in poor Melillo's glove. His phobia was well known throughout the league and it made him a constant target for pranksters like Rowe.

Oscar ran out there, put his glove on, felt something hairy, and tossed his glove about 20 feet in the air. He started yelling and screaming.

"What the hell's the matter with you?" asked Joe Cronin, the player/manager for the Red Sox.

"There's something in my glove," Melillo said. "There's some kind of animal in there. Get that thing out of there."

Cronin came over and looked at the glove. "What are you talking about?" he said. "There isn't anything in there."

"Yes, there is," Melillo said. "Put your hand in there and you'll see." Cronin took a closer look and found the dead bird.

Boots Poffenberger's name also tends to surface a lot when we're swapping stories. I'll never forget the day we were in Washington and the game was delayed by rain. They covered the field and when they took that cover off it was just like a steam oven. It was particularly hot and muggy that day. When the game resumed, Poffenberger went out there to start the inning. We didn't have any other pitcher loosening up. Cochrane was sitting back there catching and sweat was pouring off of him by the gallon. All at once, Boots started walking off the mound toward the dugout on the third-base side.

Sitting on his haunches, Cochrane hollered, "Where the hell are you going, Boots?"

"I'm going to the clubhouse," Boots answered. "It's too hot to pitch." Boots kept right on walking into the clubhouse. Cochrane suspended him, sat him down for a week or so. Cochrane was always game to tell a good baseball story, but I don't think he thought that one was very funny.

The late Gil English wouldn't laugh at this next story. But I guarantee you he would blush.

English was a teammate of mine with the Tigers. He was a very straight arrow, a proper gentleman. He had just joined us, and might have been eager to prove that he was one of the boys and could fit right in.

One day he was playing catch with somebody in front of the dugout, loosening up before taking infield practice. He looked up in the stands, five rows behind our dugout, and a gal up there reading the newspaper caught his eye. She had her legs crossed and you could see about four or five inches above her knee, which was quite a bit in those days.

"Hey, you want to see a cute little ass?" he asked.

"Sure," I said. After all, there is no law against looking.

"Look right behind you, about the fifth row up," he said.

"Hey, that's pretty nice," I replied.

"I'll say," English said.

"You want to know something, Gil?" I asked. "I slept with her last night."

His face lit up with amazement. "You're kidding," he said. "Did you really?"

"That's right," I said. "That's my wife."

His face turned redder than a tomato. "Oh my God, all the people in the ballpark and I've got to pick your wife out to say something about," he said. "I'm very sorry."

"That's OK, Gil," I said. "You've got no reason to be sorry. I agree with everything you said. It's all true."

Chapter 23

Good-Bye Old Girl

The headline "Auker Says Good-Bye to Old Girl" jumped off the page of the *Vero Beach Press Journal* sports section and grabbed the attention of our housekeeper. She waited until I left the room and sidled up to Mildred with an expression made up of part sympathy and part admiration of Mildred's strength. She wanted Mildred to know she had a friend in her time of need.

"Who was she?" Darlene whispered, and then braced herself for an explanation of the apparent scandal. Darlene thought the "old girl" in the headline was some old flame of mine.

In reality, the old girl the headline referred to was Tiger Stadium, put to sleep in 1999 after housing 88 years of baseball history at the corner of Michigan and Trumbull. Our local paper ran a story on my involvement in the closing ceremonies for the ballpark.

I talked over the telephone many times to a nice young woman who was involved in arranging for the former players to partake in the closing ceremonies. "I want to thank you so much for all the help you've given me, Mr. Auker," she said. "If you don't mind, there is one more thing I'd like you to help me with. I was wondering if you could help me locate Mr. Mickey Cochrane and Mr. Ty Cobb," she said sweetly.

Evidently, she wasn't much of a baseball fan; I had to inform her that Mr. Cochrane and Mr. Cobb had passed away.

I was asked to speak at the ceremonies because I'm the ex-player with the most seniority. Brad Ausmus, the Tigers' catcher and captain, represented the current-day Tigers. More than 60 players formed a chronologically ordered line that started at home plate and stretched all the way to the flagpole in center field. The flag with the Detroit Tiger logo was lowered and passed from me at one end of the line to Ausmus at the other.

Talking into a microphone in front of the packed crowd that remained after the Tigers defeated the Kansas City Royals, 8–2, in the final game played at the stadium, I said:

> Brad, take this flag to Comerica Park, your new home, and take with it the boyhood dreams, the perseverance, and the competitive desire it takes to become a Detroit Tiger. Never forget us, for we live on by those that carry on the Tiger tradition and who so proudly wear the Olde English D. To wear this uniform is a great privilege and an honor. On behalf of the old Tigers, we ask the young Tigers of today and tomorrow to wear this uniform with pride and never on the field or off allow your personal conduct to defile or disgrace the great tradition this uniform represents. And always remember, Brad, once a Tiger, always a Tiger. Thank you and God bless all the Tigers of the past, the present, and the future, and God bless the fans who make this all possible.

After the ceremony was over, we changed out of our uniforms and into our civilian clothes. We had a police escort waiting for us. There must have been a thousand fans waiting for us to come

The old girl—Tigers Stadium, also known as Briggs Stadium. *Photo courtesy of the Associated Press.*

out. There were so many people wanting autographs, we never would have been able to get out of the place without that escort.

I was the next-to-last one to walk out and Ron LeFlore, the popular, base-stealing outfielder from the 1970s, walked out just before I did. As soon as LeFlore walked out in front of all those people, two police officers handcuffed him, walked him through the crowd, and took him to the county jail, where he spent the night. Oh well, so much for my speech.

I felt so sorry for him. I think the police could have found a better way to handle that. He was arrested for failure to pay more than $50,000 in back child support. He said he couldn't make the payments because his only income was a $20,000 annual pension from baseball.

LeFlore received a big ovation during the ceremonies and was always a fan favorite because of his rise from the depths of prison to the heights of Tiger stardom. The Tigers had discovered LeFlore playing baseball as an inmate at Jackson State Prison in Michigan. His chance to enjoy one more night as a star, worshipped by the baseball fans of Detroit, was cut short in an unceremonious manner.

Four members of the Tigers' first World Championship in 1935 were still alive as the twenty-first century began. Ray Hayworth, Billy Rogell, and Chief Hogsett join Elden Auker on that list.

Hayworth lives in an assisted-care residence in Thomasville, North Carolina, and enjoys watching his grandson, J. D. Hayworth, a Republican congressman from Arizona, make appearances on various political television talk shows.

Hogsett lives in a rest home in Ellis, Kansas, and, sadly, suffers from Alzheimer's Disease. According to Auker, "Babe Ruth couldn't hit Chief Hogsett with a handful of sand."

Billy Rogell lives in a rest home in Detroit after serving as a city councilman for several decades. Many of his constituents have played in the local Little League named after him, which made him a tough political opponent to beat. The street leading to the airport in Detroit is named Billy Rogell Drive.

Auker asked Rogell how he liked where he was living and was told he didn't like it. "What's the matter, Billy, don't you have a nice place?" Auker asked.

"No, it's not that," Rogell said. "It's beautiful."

"Don't you like the food?" Auker asked.

"No, it's not that," Rogell said. "The food's great."

"What don't you like about it?" Auker asked.

"Too many old people," said Rogell. He was 96 at the time.

Other than that sad incident involving LeFlore, it was a memorable night packed with emotion for all in attendance.

I stammered at one point during my speech because I noticed tears running down the cheeks of Ernie Harwell, the great Tigers broadcaster who had witnessed so many legendary moments at the corner of Michigan and Trumbull. It really flustered me when I saw that, and I had trouble finding my place again. Harwell was so emotional, but he wasn't the only one. George Kell was crying too. In fact, many of the players were crying.

Harwell stepped to the microphone. More than 40,000 people took comfort in the words spoken by the beloved voice of the Tigers. "Tonight we say good-bye," Harwell said. "But we will not forget. Open your eyes, take a look around, and take a mental picture. Moments like this will live on."

Harwell's final call from Tiger Stadium will be played over and over: "Tigers lead it 8–2. Two down in the ninth inning. Jones is ready. He delivers. Here's a swing and a miss. The game is over, and Tiger Stadium is no more."

All night long, the air was filled with talk of great moments from bygone eras. They talked of Babe Ruth's 1926 home run, which legend has it traveled 626 feet. They talked of Kirk Gibson's takeout slides, Al Kaline's throws from right field, George Kell's batting title, double plays turned by Billy Rogell and Charlie Gehringer, and the twin killings authored by Alan Trammell and Lou Whitaker. They talked of the home run Ted Williams hit in 1941 to win the All-Star Game for the American League, Hank Greenberg's home run upon his return from four years of military service, Denny McLain's 31-win season, big-bellied Mickey Lolich's World Series heroics, and Mark "the Bird" Fidrych's histrionics. I thought back to Goose Goslin, sprinting through the sea of bodies, hollering, "What'd I tell ya? What'd I tell ya?"

Said Dennis Archer, mayor of Detroit, "The great times we've experienced in Tiger Stadium we'll cherish forever. Now, let's create some new memories in Comerica Park."

Every time a speaker mentioned Comerica Park, the crowd booed loudly, an indication that some of the great baseball fans of Detroit weren't ready to say good-bye to the ballpark that opened as Navin Field on April 20, 1912, and became Briggs Stadium in 1938. They were booing with their hearts, not their heads.

It was time for the Tigers to move into a new home. They brought me in for the opener of Comerica Park in 2000. It's a beautiful stadium, a definite upgrade. The same flag that was passed from center field to home plate at Tiger Stadium was passed from home plate to center field at Comerica Park, where Brad Ausmus and I raised it on the flagpole.

Ernie was right when he said Tiger Stadium will live forever in our memories. But I'm not such a hypocrite as to bemoan the stadium's replacement. Who am I to complain about progress? After all, I'm on my fourth pacemaker.

Chapter 24

Betty Co-Ed

I didn't have a date for the varsity dance on the eve of my college graduation, so I went stag. As the dance was winding down, a group of my fellow athletes suggested I get a date and join them for an after-the-dance cookout at a park. They planned to grill hamburgers and roast weenies and marshmallows.

I was voted Joe College our senior year at Kansas State and Mildred was voted Betty Co-Ed, but we never had gone out on a date. Mildred had come to the dance with Doc Kennedy, an old grade school and high school classmate of hers who was studying to become a veterinarian.

While the two of us danced, I asked Mildred if she would like to join me for the cookout. "I'm with Doc," she said. "He picked me up at the house and my folks would expect him to bring me back. I really don't think I can go."

My first pitch didn't work, so I tried another.

"If I had your folks' permission, would you go?" I asked.

"Well, I suppose I would, yes," Mildred said.

It was about 11:00 P.M. Without Mildred's knowledge, I got on the phone and called her mother. I knew her very well because Mildred's brother, Morris Purcell, was a fraternity brother of mine.

"Sorry to wake you, Mrs. Purcell," I said. "This is Elden. I'm calling from the varsity dance. A bunch of the guys are going to take their dates out for a second date to have a cookout. I was wondering if it would be all right with you if I took Mildred."

"It's fine with me if she wants to go," Mrs. Purcell said. "She'll have to work it out with Doc, though."

I found Mildred and made one more pitch. "I just called your mom," I told her.

"You what?" she said with shock. "Did you wake her up?"

"You told me if I got your parents' permission you would go with me," I persisted. "She said it's OK with her as long as you could settle it with Doc. Can you tell Doc?"

She did, and we went out. I didn't bring her home until about 4:00 A.M.

It pays to be persistent. It won't be long before we're celebrating our 70th wedding anniversary.

We both turned ninety in 2000, and we remain a two-car family. That way she can get to her bridge games without bumming a ride when I'm out on the golf course. I'm the better golfer. Mildred's the better cribbage player. She keeps a little sheet tucked away in the cribbage game and tallies what I owe her. We play for 10 cents a game, one penny a peg. I owe her $11.60. Yesterday I owed her $11.30. She's going to break me yet. Mildred sets aside her bridge winnings and drops them into the Sunday collection basket. We call it the Lord's money.

Clifford, the tubby yellow lab from next door, will be by shortly to go through his daily routine. One by one, I feed him a handful of Milk-Bones. He knows he must shake hands to earn the second-to-the-last one, and shake hands he does. He knows he won't get the very last one unless he walks down the steps of the pool and takes a quick swim, so into the pool he walks. After his short swim, he shakes himself off and heads back home to watch over the children.

Mildred Purcell, in uniform as honorary colonel of the 1931 ROTC Dance. *Photo from the personal collection of Elden Auker.*

One at a time, the three children who are under Clifford's watch also stop by. Back at their house, the middle child spots the oldest with a cookie and knows where to go to get one for herself. Then the baby spots his sister with a cookie, and he too knows where to go. Little Christopher, wearing a T-shirt and a diaper, holds a bottle filled with juice in one hand and, without saying a word, patiently waits, free hand raised, in front of the cookie jar. They're another generation of Americans weaned on Oreo cookies, which, like baseball, are an American tradition that has stood the test of time.

Baseball careers and Oreo cookies have short shelf lives. They vanish before you realize it. Man cannot live on baseball and Oreos alone. Anyone who tries to do so is bound for disappointment.

Listen closely and you can hear the beautiful lilt of Mildred's voice coming from out back. She is engaged in her morning ritual, feeding her favorite great blue heron, calling "Lil' Blue, Lil' Blue." Save for the hip that throws her gait off balance just a touch, she looks no different to me than the young lady I dated with the permission of her mother on graduation eve so many years ago (to the chagrin of poor Doc Kennedy).

Mildred's beckoning words to Lil' Blue are as unnecessary to the animal as they are soothing to me. She has been feeding him since he left the nest. Like one of Pavlov's dogs, the great blue heron starts its flight the instant it hears the click of the screen door handle. It leaves the bank on the other side of one of the five deep-water canals hooked up to the Indian River. In that canal mullet jump, trout swim, and every so often a porpoise cruises by, spitting water. The great blue heron climbs with the grace of Joe DiMaggio running down a flyball in the gap, and makes its way high above the canal with the power of Jimmie Foxx connecting with a fastball. Its awesome wingspan stretches from left field to right field. In flight, it appears invincible. It lands and tucks its wings; on the ground it suddenly seems

Elden and Mildred Auker in 1989. *Photo from the personal collection of Elden Auker.*

vulnerable, with its scrawny legs, pencil neck, and uncertainty about each awkward step.

Lil' Blue gathers the pieces of raw meat Mildred has sprinkled onto the grass. Today's breakfast is uncooked bacon. Yesterday's was raw hamburger.

Soon, Lil' Blue is back in flight, one more of its precious days on earth enriched by the nurturing hand of my dear Mildred.

Index